Collectibles 101™

Fast Food Toys

Joyce & Terry Losonsky

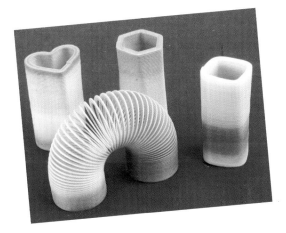

Schiffer Publishing Ltd®

4880 Lower Valley Road, Atglen, PA 19310 USA

Dedication

We would like to dedicate this book to all our collector friends who have followed their passion and collected fast food toys just for the fun of it! The treasure hunt for these toys is an experience that can last a lifetime! As cherished as the toys are, the memories and FUN collected along the way may be the most cherished collectible of all.

Copyright © 1999 by Joyce and Terry Losonsky
Library of Congress Catalog Card Number: 99-64414

All rights reserved. No part of this work may be reproduced or used in any form or by any means—graphic, electronic, or mechanical, including photocopying or information storage and retrieval systems—without written permission from the copyright holder.

"Schiffer," "Schiffer Publishing Ltd. & Design," and the "Design of pen and ink well" are registered trademarks of Schiffer Publishing Ltd.

Designed by "Sue"
Type set in Futura Hv BT/Souvenir Lt BT

ISBN: 0-7643-0965-X
Printed in China
1 2 3 4

Published by Schiffer Publishing Ltd.
4880 Lower Valley Road
Atglen, PA 19310
Phone: (610) 593-1777; Fax: (610) 593-2002
E-mail: Schifferbk@aol.com
Please visit our web site catalog at
www.schifferbooks.com

This book may be purchased from the publisher.
Include $3.95 for shipping.
Please try your bookstore first.
We are interested in hearing from authors
with book ideas on related subjects.
You may write for a free catalog.

In Europe, Schiffer books are distributed by
Bushwood Books
6 Marksbury Rd.
Kew Gardens
Surrey TW9 4JF England
Phone: 44 (0)181 392-8585; Fax: 44 (0)181
392-9876
E-mail: Bushwd@aol.com

Contents

Acknowledgments

We especially would like to thank the following individuals for their contributions to this book: Ken Clee, Mark Carder, Eileen and Ron Corbett, Jimmy and Pat Futch, Bill and Pat Poe, E.J. Ritter, Bill Thomas, Rich and Laurel Seidelman, Pat Sentell, Brian Jones, Daman Carr, John and Eleanor Larsen, Janice Antone, Jenny Acker, Ken Brady, Ron and Ethel Bacon, Russell Better, Jr., Jon Hunter, Mary Kirby, Conrad and Nancy Kiser, Eleanor Marshall, Doug and Glenda Reading, Aaron Zeamer, Bill and Marie Boyce, Bob and MaryAnn Brown, Harvey and Cleo Bradstreet, Gerald and Helen Buchholz, Jim Challenger, Tom Challenger, Scott Chandler, Deborah Chitester, Jim and Sally Christoffel, Maynard and Patricia Carney, Scott and Susan Chandler, Ann and Cal Clark, John and Brenda Clark, David Epstein, Kathy Clark, Mary and Ron Colwell, Chris Rucho, Eva Cook, Terry and Bud Beedie, Mike and Deanna Fountaine, Mark and Carol Gillette, Lance Golba, Gary and Teena Greenberg, Linda and Jim Gegorski, Martha Gragg, Roger Hordines, Barbara Hunt, Gary and Judy Heald, Gary and Shirley Henriques, Roger Hordines, Sharon Iranpour, Dave Johnson, Joyce Klassen, Don Wilson, Robert Lanier, Tom and Terry Nelson, Teresa and Tom Olszeski, Jane Prussiano, Jerry and Lorraine Soltis, Mary Lou Souders, Barbara and Erwin Schulz, Vicky Sartin, Fran Turey, Ed Vogler, Louise and Dudley DeCastro, Luc Delaney, Leah and Robert Dobyne, Darlene and John Drew, Les Fein, Greg MacClaren, Sharon Karpiak, Sharon and Jim Jarrett, Brad and Tonya Lawing, Bill and Betty McCormick, Frank Forry, Glen and Kathleen McElwee, Mike Murphy, Maria Meltzer, Jay and Mimi Morgan, Alan and Jackie Roark, Brenda Pacamonti, Neal Reinhardt, Martha Gragg, Karen and Janet Scholtens, Essie Saunders, Bob Serighino, Jim Silva, Trudy Slaven, Jerry and Lorraine Soltis, David Stone, Frances Turey, Gary and Jill Turner, Lee Turpin, David Tuttle, Cindy Wagen, Robert Wilkey, Meredith Williams, Lloyd and Nancy Washburn, Charles and Margaret Wichmann, Rosalie Wolfe, Frank Work, Fred and Doris Huebner, Frank and Janet Zamarripa and our children: Andrea and Milton Dodge, Natasha Losonsky, Nicole and Chuck Matlach and Ryan Losonsky. May the fun of collecting and the friendships formed along the collecting trail continue for a lifetime!

Introduction
How to Have FUN Collecting

Collectibles101™: Fast Food Toys is designed to be a beginning book for collectors. Starting with toy sets given out in 1990 and ending with current sets from 1999, this book covers Kid's Meal toys from the past ten years from twenty-eight different restaurants.

Collecting all or some of these toys is a challenge and FUN! For starters, these toys can be found at neighborhood yard sales and thrift shops. The treasure hunt begins within these pages. The goal of the *Collectibles101™* series is to encourage young collectors to go out in search of FUN collecting and save for future enjoyment.

Organizing is easy. Using the Premium Numbering System, each toy is assigned a number and can be checked off, when found, as part of a set of toys. A name for the set of toys is listed at the top of the set with a number before the toy name. The numbering system represents an alphabetic label for the set and the year the set was given out, plus the number of the toy within the set. Check-off boxes are provided for marking your latest finds! One check-off column can be utilized for used toys and one column for new toys. Start with finding loose, out of package toys and check off your finds! Loose toys are more fun to enjoy, easier to arrange on shelves, easier to find, and cheaper to collect!

The FUN in collecting is trying to find all these toys at yard sales, flea markets, and about for a small amount; say, $1.00-2.00 each or less. It can be challenging, but should always be FUN! Remember, the price range listed is not the selling price—it is the price you would expect to pay a dealer for the toy. With most dealers, these toys were acquired when the value was somewhat higher than today's value. Most dealers paid more for their stock of toys and are holding them at that higher price because they believe the hobby will make a strong comeback at a time when the kids who received them for free in a Kid's Meal will begin to collect. These Kid's Meal toys represent Americana and FUN memories from one's childhood.

Toy price range listed is what you would expect to pay a dealer or pay at a toy show for the toy mint in package or in very good condition (i.e., it is not the price you would expect to obtain if you sold the toy to a dealer). The value of a loose, out of the package toy is less than the lowest value listed in the given price range. Sometimes, you may find that the cost of obtaining a toy is less than the book's designated price range for the toy and, at times, considerably more than the range given. Toy prices vary. Most dealers will not part with a toy for less than $2.00. If you go to a toy show and someone is liquidating, you could get lucky and pay less for a group of toys. But, the general rule of thumb is: a Kid's Meal toy will cost approximately $2.00-3.50 to acquire at a toy show. Today's buying price is at a great level! Kid's Meal toys, from 28 different fast food restaurants, are relatively cheap and available to collect. So, the time to begin collecting is now!

In the end, the price of an item is determined between the buyer and the seller. Currently, there is an over supply of Kid's Meal toys on the market, and it is typical for dealers to pay 30-40% of the lowest price listed in this book, in the best of selling conditions. Thus, the selling price is considerably less than the price in the range listed. The buying price can be considerably less if one is willing to join the treasure hunt for these toys. Toys should be collected today for future investment, capital gain, enjoyment, and FUN! Buying them now and putting them away for the future is the best plan. Again, remember, the goal of this *Collectibles101* ® series is to encourage young collectors to go in search of FUN collecting and to save for future enjoyment. Along the collecting way, "Having FUN while you collect" is the golden rule.

Collecting Just For Fun!

A. Why Collect—for FUN!
   For trade with other collectors
   For future value

B. Where to Collect
   School
   Yard sales
   Secondhand shops
   From friends
   Family toy box
   Thrift shops
   Buy them from fast food
      restaurants
   Relative's toy boxes

C. When to Collect—Any time!
   Free time
   Play time

D. What to Collect—Collect toys
      you enjoy!
   Collect clean loose toys
   Collect new toys (MIP—mint
      in package)
   Collect individual toys
   Collect sets of toys

E. What To Do With Toys
   Play with them
   Display them in your room
   Display them at your school
   Display them at your library
   Display them at club meetings
      (such as the Boy or Girl Scouts)
   Display them at the office
   Trade them with friends
      and family

F. How to keep toys not on display
   Store them in clean boxes
   Store them in plastic bags
   Mark your toys with set names

F. Who Collects—EVERYONE!

G. Are there collectors who sell and buy
      toys?—Yes, contact:
   Pat Sentell, 720 Biscayne Dr., Orange
      City, FL 32763 (904-775-0150)
   Ken Clee, P.O. Box 11412, Philadelphia,
      PA 19111 (212-722-1979)
   Bill Poe, 220 Dominica Circle E, Niceville,
      FL 32578 (904-897-4163)
   E. J. Ritter, 6803 Idaho Ave., Hammond,
      IN 46323 (219-844-0111)

DE Sq9101-06

Helpful Information for Using this Book

Price Information

Price range listed is the price you could expect to pay a dealer at a toy show for the toy in MIP (mint in package) condition.
Loose toys are valued at least 50% off lowest price listed in the given range.

Name and Numbering System

Premium Name: The premiums are listed by the names on the packaging whenever possible.
Premium Number (The numbering system is based on the following):
    Prefix: Restaurant name abbreviated (2 digits)
    Suffix: Alphabetic name for promotion (2 digits)

      Year of promotion (2 digits)
      Number of toy (2 digits)

Example: AR Fp9001

      Arby's = AR
      Finger Puppets = Fp
      Year = 90
      Toy = 01

Collecting Language

MIP = Mint in package.
U-3 = Toys designed for children 0+ to 3.
Toyland = an imaginary place where all collectors live and play; a playland area; a place in the hearts of all collectors.
Regional = geographical distribution was limited to specific cities, states, stores or marketing areas.
Self-Liquidator = item intended to be sold over the counter; could or could not be included in the Kid's Meal program.
Clean-up Week = open time period when no specific premium is distributed.

Arby' s

Arby's is a national fast food chain that started a kid's meal program in 1986 with Arby's Adventure Meals. Using themes based on a series of characters for eighteen months to two years for each specific promotion like Babar' s World Tour, Arby's Adventure Meal has been successful.

Arby's has achieved their success by specializing in thin-sliced roast beef sandwiches for the adult market while catering to the children's market with hamburgers. This uniquely defined target market has adequately positioned Arby's in the fast food race for consumer dollars. By not limiting promotions to four weeks, Arby's has been able to sustain its steady growth pattern by differentiating food selections and kid's meal premiums.

1980s Arby's sign

AR Babar's World Tour Finger Puppets Adventure Meal, 1990

❑ ❑	AR Fp9001	Fp: King Babar w/ camera	$2.00-3.00
❑ ❑	AR Fp9002	Fp: Arthur & Zephir	$2.00-3.00
❑ ❑	AR Fp9003	Fp: Pom w/ binoculars	$2.00-3.00
❑ ❑	AR Fp9004	Fp: Queen Celeste w/ purse	$2.00-3.00

AR Fp9001-03

AR Babar's World Tour Racers Adventure Meal, 1992

❑ ❑	AR Br9201	Cousin Arthur: in yellow car	$3.00-4.00
❑ ❑	AR Br9202	King Babar: in red car	$3.00-4.00
❑ ❑	AR Br9203	Queen Celeste: in green car	$3.00-4.00

AR Br9201-03

AR Yogi & Friends Fun Squirters Adventure Meal, 1994

❏ ❏	AR Sq9401	Character Squirter: Boo-Boo w/ ice cream	$2.00-3.00
❏ ❏	AR Sq9402	Character Squirter: Cindy Bear w/ camera	$2.00-3.00
❏ ❏	AR Sq9403·	Character Squirter: Yogi w/ picnic basket	$2.00-3.00

AR Sp9401-03

AR Yogi & Friends Snow Domes Adventure Meal, 1995

❏ ❏	AR Do9501	Snow Dome: Cindy Bear on pink base	$4.00-5.00
❏ ❏	AR Do9502	Snow Dome: Snagglepuss on blue base	$4.00-5.00
❏ ❏	AR Do9503	Snow Dome: Yogi on green base	$4.00-5.00

AR Do9501-03

AR Yogi & Friends Fun Tracer Puzzles Adventure Meal, 1996

- ❏ ❏ AR Tr9601 Character Puzzle Piece: Yogi, Cindy Bear, Boo-Boo, & Ranger Smith on pink board $2.00-3.00
- ❏ ❏ AR Tr9602 Character Puzzle Piece: Huckleberry, Quick Draw, & Snagglepuss on yellow board $2.00-3.00

AR Tr9601-02

AR Monster-Doh Adventure Meal, 1997

❏ ❏	AR Do9701	Play-doh: Dracula	$2.00-3.00
❏ ❏	AR Do9702	Play-doh: Frankenstein	$2.00-3.00
❏ ❏	AR Do9703	Play-doh: Mummy	$2.00-3.00
❏ ❏	AR Do9704	Play-doh: Werewolf	$2.00-3.00

AR Do9701-04

Big Boy

Big Boy celebrated their 60th year in 1998! Originating in Ohio as Frisch's Big Boy of Cleveland, they began their franchise in 1938. In the beginning, franchises were sold on a geographical basis: Elias Brothers in Michigan, Frisch's in Ohio, Shoney's in the southern states, and Bob's in Virginia, Maryland, and the District of Columbia (D.C.). During the nineties, Frisch's sold their franchise to the Marriott Corporation and Marriott sold their fast food segment to various other corporations. This spin-off began in the early nineties and continued in many geographical areas until Big Boy seemed not to exist in some markets. With the consolidation of franchises strengthening their marketing position, Big Boy selectively locates their restaurants on interstate highway systems rather than in local communities—appealing to customers who prefer a served meal, rather than "on the go" food. Through it all, Big Boy continued to offer toys in their kid's meal programs, sometimes emphasizing their own characters: Big Boy, Dolly, and Nugget, their dog. Some toys were available for years. The longest running premium is undoubtedly the Big Boy's Comic series, known to number in the hundreds. Big Boy's latest premium in 1998, a set of Yo-Yos, illustrates their long-standing "old timey" approach to kid's meal toys and business. Big Boy's kid's meal is simply called the "Fun Meal."

1980s Big Boy Bank

BB Doodletop Jr. Fun Meal, 1996

☐ ☐	BB Do9601	Doodle Top: purple		$1.00-2.00
☐ ☐	BB Do9602	Doodle Top: green		$1.00-2.00
☐ ☐	BB Do9603	Doodle Top: pink		$1.00-2.00
☐ ☐	BB Do9604	Doodle Top: blue		$1.00-2.00

BB Do9601-04

BB Jammin' with Big Boy Fun Meal, 1997

❏ ❏ BB Ja9701 Basketball w/ hoop & backboard
$3.00-4.00

BB Ja9701

BB Big Boy Yo-Yo Fun Meal, 1998

❏	❏	BB Yo9801	Yo-Yo: turquoise	$4.00-5.00
❏	❏	BB Yo9802	Yo-Yo: purple	$4.00-5.00
❏	❏	BB Yo9803	Yo-Yo: yellow	$4.00-5.00
❏	❏	BB Yo9804	Yo-Yo: green	$4.00-5.00
❏	❏	BB Yo9805	Yo-Yo: pink	$4.00-5.00

BB Yo9801-05

Burger King

Burger King Corporation was founded by James W. McLamore and David Edgerton, who opened their first Burger King restaurant in Miami, Florida, in 1954—one full year ahead of Ray Kroc and the McDonald's Corporation! In 1954, Burger King used the King on a Bun as their company logo. Their slogan was: "Join the Swing to Burger King."

The operation grew slowly into a chain of 274 restaurants by 1967, when it became a subsidiary entirely owned by The Pillsbury Company. At that time, the logo was changed to the short, squatty cartoon character King. By 1973, the company decided a pudgy King no longer represented the health conscious consumer, so the New King and his Royal Cast were unveiled: tall and thin. During 1973-74, the New King was shown as more of a "real person" who even did tricks!

During the late 1970s and early 1980s, Burger King advertised on radio and TV, and in newspapers and magazines with slogans like: "The Bigger the Burger the Better the Burger" (1968); "It Takes Two Hands to Handle a Whooper" (1970); "Have It Your Way" (1974); "Make It Special, Make It Burger King" (1980); and "Aren't You Hungry for Burger King Now?" (1982). Then Pillsbury was absorbed by a corporate conglomerate called the "Grand Metropolitan." The King was killed off—only the bun halves remained as the logo. As the eighties faded into the beat of the nineties generation of fast food consumers, the Burger King "King" ceased to exist.

By the 1990s, Burger King was a unit of the London-based conglomerate Diageo and had some 7,600 restaurants in the United States, compared to McDonald's 13,000+ U.S. eateries. Burger King's promotional efforts included a "Kids Club," which was introduced in 1990. When kids joined the mail-in club, they received a membership card and a newsletter sent every two months. The articles in the *Kids Club Magazine* were written by a group of cartoon characters who made up the club.

Each of the original seven club characters was designed to appeal to a certain type of child. The leader, "Kid Vid," likes computer/video games and magic. He carries his remote controller everywhere and uses it to ZAP himself and the other kids to all kinds of places. The blond-headed girl, "Snaps," the reporter of the group, loves taking pictures and carries a camera everywhere. "Jaws" (always talking or "jawing") is an African-American boy who loves the environment and is concerned about recycling. The child genius of the group is "I.Q." (Intelligence Quotient), who wears glasses and is the shortest child. "Lingo" (from the Latin word *lingus* meaning "language") is a bilingual boy who speaks both English and Spanish and is the artist of the group. "Wheels" is the boy with the high-performance wheelchair who loves anything mechanical. The last member of the original group is "Boomer" (whenever she kicks a soccer ball you hear a big "boom"), a red-headed girl who is devoted to all types of sports. Burger King's meal for children is called a "Kids Club Meal."

In late the 1990s, Burger King added two additional characters to their "Kids Club." They are "J.D.," the club's dog, and "Jazz," an Oriental friend. These additional characters expanded the Burger King Kids Club character lineup to nine characters.

1990s Burger King sign

BK Lickety Splits Rolling Racers Kids Club Meal, 1990

❏ ❏	BK Li9001	Carbo Cooler drink	$2.00-3.00
❏ ❏	BK Li9002	Carsan'wich croissant	$2.00-3.00
❏ ❏	BK Li9003	Chicken Chassis chicken nugget	$2.00-3.00
❏ ❏	BK Li9004	Expresstix french toast	$2.00-3.00
❏ ❏	BK Li9005	Flame Broiled Buggy hamburger	$2.00-3.00
❏ ❏	BK Li9006	Indianapolis race car apple pie	$2.00-3.00
❏ ❏	BK Li9007	Spry Fries french fries	$2.00-3.00

BK Li9001-07

BK Simpsons Kids Club Meal, 1990

❑ ❑	BK Si9001	Bart w/ backpack		$2.00-4.00
❑ ❑	BK Si9002	Homer waving w/ blue hat		$2.00-4.00
❑ ❑	BK Si9003	Lisa w/ saxophone		$2.00-4.00
❑ ❑	BK Si9004	Maggie on turtle		$2.00-4.00
❑ ❑	BK Si9005	Marge w/ birds in hair		$2.00-4.00

BK Si9001-05

BK Archies Vehicles Kids Club Meal, 1991

❑ ❑	BK Ve9101	Archie in red car		$4.00-5.00
❑ ❑	BK Ve9102	Betty in blue car		$4.00-5.00
❑ ❑	BK Ve9103	Jughead in green car		$4.00-5.00
❑ ❑	BK Ve9104	Veronica in purple car		$4.00-5.00

BK Ve9101-04

BK Beauty & the Beast Kids Club Meal, 1991

☐ ☐ BK Be9101   Belle $2.00-4.00
☐ ☐ BK Be9102   Chip, the Cup $3.00-5.00
☐ ☐ BK Be9103   Cogsworth, the Clock $3.00-5.00
☐ ☐ BK Be9104   The Beast $2.00-4.00

BK Be9101-04

BK Go-Go Gadget Gizmos Kids Club Meal, 1991

☐ ☐ BK Ga9101   Copter Gadget w/ red blades/2p $3.00-4.00
☐ ☐ BK Ga9102   Inflated Gadget $3.00-4.00
☐ ☐ BK Ga9103   Scuba Gadget w/ orange fins/3p $3.00-4.00
☐ ☐ BK Ga9104   Surfer Gadget w/ grn board/sail/3p $3.00-4.00

BK Ga9101-04

BK Aladdin Kids Club Meal, 1992

❑ ❑	BK Al9201	Abu		$2.00-3.00
❑ ❑	BK Al9202	Aladdin & Magic Carpet/2p		$2.00-3.00
❑ ❑	BK Al9203	Genie & the Lamp		$2.00-3.00
❑ ❑	BK Al9204	Jasmine & Rajah/2p		$2.00-3.00
❑ ❑	BK Al9205	Jafar & Iago		$2.00-3.00

BK Al9201-05

BK Goof Troop Bowlers Kids Club Meal, 1992

❑ ❑	BK Go9201	Goofy w/ orange shirt		$2.00-3.00
❑ ❑	BK Go9202	Max w/ red shirt		$2.00-3.00
❑ ❑	BK Go9203	Pete w/ green shirt		$2.00-3.00
❑ ❑	BK Go9204	PJ w/ blue shirt		$2.00-3.00

BK
Go9201-04

BK Glow-In-The-Dark Trolls Kids Club Meal, 1993

❏ ❏	BK Gl9301	I.Q. w/ orange hair	$1.00-3.00
❏ ❏	BK Gl9302	Jaws w/ green hair	$1.00-3.00
❏ ❏	BK Gl9303	Kid Vid w/ purple hair	$1.00-3.00
❏ ❏	BK Gl9304	Snaps w/ yellow hair	$1.00-3.00

BK Gl9301-04

BK Little Mermaid Splash Collection Kids Club Meal, 1993

❏ ❏	BK Me9301	Ariel on Turtle wind-up	$2.00-4.00
❏ ❏	BK Me9302	Flounder squirter	$2.00-4.00
❏ ❏	BK Me9303	Sebastian Crab wind-up	$2.00-4.00
❏ ❏	Bk Me9304	Urchin Seahorse squirt gun	$2.00-4.00

BK Me9301-04

BK Lion King I Kids Club Meal, 1994

❏ ❏	BK Li9401	Simba: Baby Lion	$2.00-4.00
❏ ❏	BK Li9402	Pumbaa & Timon	$2.00-4.00
❏ ❏	BK Li9403	Nala	$2.00-4.00
❏ ❏	BK Li9404	Rafiki: Baboon	$2.00-4.00
❏ ❏	BK Li9405	Scar	$2.00-4.00
❏ ❏	BK Li9406	Mafusa: Lion King	$2.00-4.00
❏ ❏	BK Li9407	Ed the Hyena	$2.00-4.00

BK Li9401-07

BK Sports Figures Kids Club Meal, 1994

❏ ❏	BK Sp9401	Boomer: Ice Hockey	$1.00-3.00
❏ ❏	BK Sp9402	I.Q.: Flying Disk	$1.00-3.00
❏ ❏	BK Sp9403	Jaws: Football	$1.00-3.00
❏ ❏	BK Sp9404	Snaps: Soccer Ball	$1.00-3.00
❏ ❏	BK Sp9405	Kid Vid: Basketball	$1.00-3.00

BK Sp9401-05

BK Toy Story I Kids Club Meal, 1995

❏ ❏	BK To9501	Buzz Lightyear		$2.00-4.00
❏ ❏	BK To9502	Racing R.C. Car		$2.00-4.00
❏ ❏	BK To9503	Army Recon Squad: 4 soldiers		$2.00-4.00
❏ ❏	BK To9504	Mr. Potato Head		$2.00-4.00
❏ ❏	BK To9505	Rex		$2.00-4.00
❏ ❏	BK To9506	Woody		$2.00-4.00

BK To9501-06

BK Lion King Finger Puppets II Kids Club Meal, 1995

❏ ❏	BK Lk9501	Fp: Rafiki (blue)		$2.00-4.00
❏ ❏	BK Lk9502	Fp: Simba (orange)		$2.00-4.00
❏ ❏	BK Lk9503	Fp: Mufasa (blue)		$2.00-4.00
❏ ❏	BK Lk9504	Fp: Ed (maroon)		$2.00-4.00
❏ ❏	BK Lk9505	Fp: Scar (purple)		$2.00-4.00
❏ ❏	BK Lk9506	Fp: Pumbaa (green)		$2.00-4.00

BK Lk9501-06

BK Pocahontas I Kids Club Meal, 1995

❏ ❏	BK Po9501	Captain John Smith	$2.00-4.00
❏ ❏	BK Po9502	Meeko (raccoon)	$2.00-4.00
❏ ❏	BK Po9503	Grandmother Willow (tree)	$2.00-4.00
❏ ❏	BK Po9504	Pocahontas	$2.00-4.00
❏ ❏	BK Po9505	Governor Ratcliffe	$2.00-4.00
❏ ❏	BK Po9506	Percy (dog)	$2.00-4.00
❏ ❏	BK Po9507	Flit (bird)	$2.00-4.00
❏ ❏	BK Po9508	Chief Powhatan	$2.00-4.00

BK Po9501-08

BK M & M I Kids Club Meal, 1996

❏ ❏	BK Mm9601	Orange Dump Truck	$2.00-4.00
❏ ❏	BK Mm9602	Blue Saxophone Player	$2.00-4.00
❏ ❏	BK Mm9603	Green "M & M" in purple car	$2.00-4.00
❏ ❏	BK Mm9604	Red "M & M" on green inner tube	$2.00-4.00
❏ ❏	BK Mm9605	Yellow "M & M" w/ lunch box	$2.00-4.00

BK Mm9601-05

BK Scooby-Doo Kids Club Meal, 1996

❑ ❑	BK Sc9601	Shaggy & Scooby Tombstone: green base	$2.00-4.00
❑ ❑	BK Sc9602	Daphne, Scooby, & Velma: racing coffin	$2.00-4.00
❑ ❑	BK Sc9603	Scooby-Doo	$2.00-4.00
❑ ❑	BK Sc9604	Shaggy/Scooby Mystery Machine	$2.00-4.00
❑ ❑	BK Sc9605	Scrappy-Doo	$2.00-4.00

BK Sc9601-05

BK Toy Story II Kids Club Meal, 1996

❑ ❑	BK To9601	Jawbreaker Scud	$2.00-4.00
❑ ❑	BK To9602	Spaced-Out Alien	$2.00-4.00
❑ ❑	BK To9603	Stroll 'N Scope Lenny	$2.00-4.00
❑ ❑	BK To9604	Speedy Deposit Hamm	$2.00-4.00
❑ ❑	BK To9605	Blast-Away Buzz Lightyear	$2.00-4.00
❑ ❑	BK To9606	Round 'Em Up Woody	$2.00-4.00
❑ ❑	BK To9607	Spin-Top Bo Peep	$2.00-4.00
❑ ❑	BK To9608	Stretch 'N Roll Slinky Dog	$2.00-4.00

BK To9601-08

BK Anastasia Kids Club Meal, 1997

❏ ❏	BK An9701	Bouncing Bartok		$2.00-3.00
❏ ❏	BK An9702	Fiendish Flyer		$2.00-3.00
❏ ❏	BK An9703	Beanie Bat Bartok		$2.00-3.00
❏ ❏	BK An9704	Anya & Pooka		$2.00-3.00
❏ ❏	BK An9705	Collision Course Dimitri		$2.00-3.00
❏ ❏	BK An9706	Fall Apart Fiend Rasputin		$2.00-3.00

BK An9701-06

BK M & M II Minis Kids Club Meal, 1997

❏ ❏	BK Mm9701	Scoop & Shoot Buggy		$1.00-3.00
❏ ❏	BK Mm9702	Giggle Stick		$1.00-3.00
❏ ❏	BK Mm9703	Chomping Teeth Swarm		$1.00-3.00
❏ ❏	BK Mm9704	Secret Swarm Squirter		$1.00-3.00
❏ ❏	BK Mm9705	Crazy Pull-Back Swarm		$1.00-3.00

BK Mm9701-05

BK Superman Kids Club Meal, 1997

❏ ❏	BK Su9701	Superman Launcher	$3.00-5.00
❏ ❏	BK Su9702	Spinning Telephone Booth	$3.00-5.00
❏ ❏	BK Su9703	Daily Planet Balancer	$3.00-5.00
❏ ❏	BK Su9704	Superman Flight Ready	$3.00-5.00
❏ ❏	BK Su9705	Lois Lane in Convertible Car	$3.00-5.00

BK Su9701-05

BK Universal Studios Monsters Kids Club Meal, 1997

❏ ❏	BK Mo9701	Down For the Count Dracula	$3.00-5.00
❏ ❏	BK Mo9702	Bolts & Volts Frankenstein	$3.00-5.00
❏ ❏	BK Mo9703	The Wolfman Cellar Dweller	$3.00-5.00
❏ ❏	BK Mo9704	The Creature Scaly Squirter	$3.00-5.00

BK Mo9701-04

BK Men in Black Kids Club Meal, 1998

❏ ❏	BK Me9801	Red Button Building Buster	$2.00-5.00
❏ ❏	BK Me9802	Red Button Loop Blaster	$2.00-5.00
❏ ❏	BK Me9803	Squishy Worm Guy	$2.00-5.00
❏ ❏	BK Me9804	Squirting Worm Guy	$2.00-5.00
❏ ❏	BK Me9805	Split Apart Light-Up Zed	$2.00-5.00
❏ ❏	BK Me9806	Split Apart Rotating Zed	$2.00-5.00
❏ ❏	BK Me9807	Slimmed Out Kay	$2.00-5.00
❏ ❏	BK Me9808	Slimmed Out Jay	$2.00-5.00
❏ ❏	BK Me9809	Neutralizer	$2.00-5.00
❏ ❏	BK Me9810	Building Space Spinner	$2.00-5.00
❏ ❏	BK Me9811	Globe Space Spinner	$2.00-5.00
❏ ❏	BK Me9812	Alien Detector	$2.00-5.00

BK Me9801-12

BK Mr. Potato Head Kids Club Meal, 1998

❏ ❏	BK Po9801	Fry Flyer	$2.00-4.00
❏ ❏	BK Po9802	Spinning Spud	$2.00-4.00
❏ ❏	BK Po9803	Hats Off Mr. Potato Head	$2.00-4.00
❏ ❏	BK Po9804	Mr. Potato Head Speedster	$2.00-4.00
❏ ❏	BK Po9805	Basket Shoot	$2.00-4.00

BK Po9801-05

BK Rugrats Kids Club Meal, 1998

❑ ❑	BK Ru9801	Hero on the Move Tommy	$3.00-4.00
❑ ❑	BK Ru9802	Jumpin' Chuckie	$3.00-4.00
❑ ❑	BK Ru9803	Wind Blown Angelica	$3.00-4.00
❑ ❑	BK Ru9804	Reptar Alive	$3.00-4.00
❑ ❑	BK Ru9805	Tandem Trekking Phil & Lil	$3.00-4.00

BK Ru9801-05

BK Small Soldiers Kids Club Meal, 1998

❑ ❑	BK Sm9801	Morning Brake Brick Bazooka: vehicle	$2.00-4.00
❑ ❑	BK Sm9802	Crawling Link Static: soldier w/ backpack/2p	$2.00-4.00
❑ ❑	BK Sm9803	Butch Battle: Frankenstein/Butch fig wind-up	$2.00-4.00
❑ ❑	BK Sm9804	Rip Roarin' Kip Killigan: blue motorcycle w/ fig attached	$2.00-4.00
❑ ❑	BK Sm9805	Nick Nitro: soldier fig w/ backpack/legs & arms detach)	$2.00-4.00
❑ ❑	BK Sm9806	Chip Hazard: soldier w/ blinking light on chest	$2.00-4.00
❑ ❑	BK Sm9807	Soft 'N Cuddly Slamfist: plush	$2.00-4.00
❑ ❑	BK Sm9808	Laughing Insaniac: spins on left arms	$2.00-4.00
❑ ❑	BK Sm9809	Levitating Lens Ocular: tripod feet	$2.00-4.00
❑ ❑	BK Sm9810	Freedom Firing Arches: arrow lights	$2.00-4.00
❑ ❑	BK Sm9811	Boulder Blasting Punch-It & Scratch-It: boulder flies	$2.00-4.00
❑ ❑	BK Sm9812	Bobbling Insaniac: purple fig spins	$2.00-4.00

BK Sm9801-12

Carl's Jr.

Carl's Jr. was a West Coast chain of fast food restaurants until 1998, when it acquired the last of the Hardee's chain of restaurants in the South. Started in 1941 and continued for more than fifty years, Carl's Jr. initially operated only in California, Oregon, Washington state, and Arizona. For the first fifty years, no kid's meal program existed. Then, in the early 1990s, the Happy Star Kid's Meal began to take shape. By 1991, the Fiftieth Anniversary of Carl's Jr., the Happy Star Meal program began in earnest. The kid's meal program currently centers around a Happy Star character, shaped like a bright yellow star, with each Happy Star Kid's Meal promotion having four or five premiums and a theme bag.

1990s Carl's Jr. DRIVE THRU sign

CJ Life Savers Roll 'Em Happy Star Kid's Meal, 1990

❏ ❏	CJ Li9001	Life Saver holder: cherry color	$4.00-7.00
❏ ❏	CJ Li9002	Life Saver holder: lemon color	$4.00-7.00
❏ ❏	CJ Li9003	Life Saver holder: lime color	$4.00-7.00
❏ ❏	CJ Li9004	Life Saver holder: orange color	$4.00-7.00
❏ ❏	CJ Li9005	Life Saver holder: yellow color	$4.00-7.00

CJ Li9001-05

CJ Flyin' Away Happy Star Kid's Meal, 1993

☐ ☐	CJ Fl9301	Airplane: High Flying Happy w/ wings	$2.00-4.00
☐ ☐	CJ Fl9302	Blimp: inflatable w/ parts of airplane flyer	$2.00-4.00
☐ ☐	CJ Fl9303	Bracelet: Flipout Flyer	$2.00-4.00
☐ ☐	CJ Fl9304	Activity Fun Book: Flight Log	$2.00-4.00

CJ Fl9301-03

CJ Shark! Happy Star Kid's Meal, 1993

❑ ❑	CJ Sh9301	Inflatable Innertube Ring	$2.00-3.00
❑ ❑	CJ Sh9302	Hammerhead Fig: purple w/ stickers	$2.00-3.00
❑ ❑	CJ Sh9303	Bubble Blower	$3.00-5.00
❑ ❑	CJ Sh9304	Cup: w/ blue shark character top	$2.00-3.00

CJ Sh9301-04

CJ Beakman's World Happy Star Kid's Meal, 1994

❑ ❑	CJ Be9401	"Elementary" Fun: changing cube	$2.00-3.00
❑ ❑	CJ Be9402	It's a Magnetic World: magnet in blue egg container	$2.00-3.00
❑ ❑	CJ Be9403	Physics Follies: rolling wheel	$2.00-3.00
❑ ❑	CJ Be9404	D' Facts of Life: yel light bulb case w/ wand	$2.00-3.00

CJ Be9401-04

CJ Chipmunk Snow Dome Sleds Happy Star Kid's Meal, 1994

❏ ❏	CJ Ch9401	Simon w/ saxophone in blue car	$4.00-6.00
❏ ❏	CJ Ch9402	Brittany in yellow car	$4.00-6.00
❏ ❏	CJ Ch9403	Alvin in pink car	$4.00-6.00
❏ ❏	CJ Ch9404	Theodore in purple car	$4.00-6.00

Comment: Cars have bubble dome top with glitter and water within the dome.

CJ Ch9401-04

CJ Star Spring Happy Star Kid's Meal, 1994

❏ ❏	CJ St9401	Slinky: star shaped/rainbow colors	$2.00-3.00

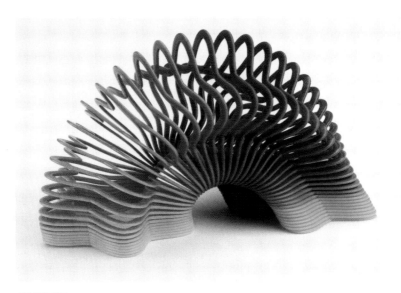

CJ St9401

CJ Life Savers Rockin' Wheelin' Kids Happy Star Kid's Meal, 1995

❏ ❏	CJ Li9501	Life Saver Container: cherry	$3.00-6.00
❏ ❏	CJ Li9502	Life Saver Container: lemon	$3.00-6.00
❏ ❏	CJ Li9503	Life Saver Container: lime	$3.00-6.00
❏ ❏	CJ Li9504	Life Saver Container: orange	$3.00-6.00
❏ ❏	CJ Li9505	Life Saver Container: pineapple	$3.00-6.00

CJ Li9501-05

CJ 100th Anniversary Tootsie Roll Train Happy Star Kid's Meal, 1996

❏ ❏	CJ An9601	Engine (red)	$4.00-8.00
❏ ❏	CJ An9602	Passenger Car (yellow)	$4.00-8.00
❏ ❏	CJ An9603	Coal Car (purple)	$4.00-8.00
❏ ❏	CJ An9604	Caboose (green)	$4.00-8.00

CJ An9601-04

CJ Garfield Happy Star Kid's Meal, 1997

❏ ❏ CJ Ga9701   Snowplow: Garfield Clearing the Way $3.00-6.00
❏ ❏ CJ Ga9702   Sledding: Garfield Slippin' & Slidin' $3.00-6.00
❏ ❏ CJ Ga9703   Snowmobile: Garfield on vehicle $3.00-6.00
❏ ❏ CJ Ga9704   Downhill Racer: Garfield on vehicle $3.00-6.00

CJ Ga9701-04

CJ Life with Louie Camping Gear Happy Star Kid's Meal, 1997

❏ ❏ CJ Li9701   Tools: red whistle/blue tweezers/ruler $2.00-3.00
❏ ❏ CJ Li9702   Canteen: blue w/ red lid $2.00-3.00
❏ ❏ CJ Li9703   Bug Box: green w/ yellow dome $2.00-3.00
❏ ❏ CJ Li9704   Compass: orange w/ belt clip $2.00-5.00

CJ Li9701-04

CJ Sonic the Hedgehog & Pals Happy Star Kid's Meal, 1997

❑ ❑	CJ So9701	Viewer: Knuckles Sticker/red	$2.00-3.00
❑ ❑	CJ So9702	Viewer: Mr. Robotnik Sticker/yellow	$2.00-3.00
❑ ❑	CJ So9703	Viewer: Sonic/Hedgehog Sticker/blue	$2.00-3.00
❑ ❑	CJ So9704	Viewer: orange	$2.00-3.00

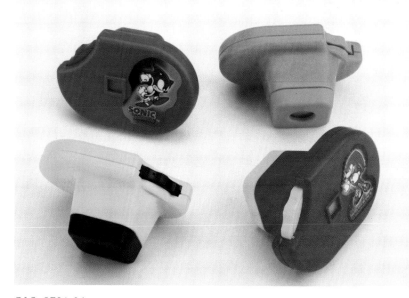

CJ So9701-04

CJ The Tick Happy Star Kid's Meal, 1997

❑ ❑ CJ Tc9701 The Tick
$2.00-4.00
❑ ❑ CJ Tc9702 Arthur
$2.00-4.00
❑ ❑ CJ Tc9703 Human Ton
$2.00-4.00
❑ ❑ CJ Tc9704 Speak
$2.00-4.00

CJ Tc9701-04

CJ Sylvester & Tweety Mysteries Happy Star Kid's Meal, 1998

❏ ❏	CJ Sy9801	Squirter: Sylvester's face	$2.00-4.00
❏ ❏	CJ Sy9802	Spin Top: Sylvester & Tweety case scene	$2.00-4.00
❏ ❏	CJ Sy9803	Runaway Chair: Sylvester & Tweety/purple	$2.00-4.00
❏ ❏	CJ Sy9804	Viewer: Tweety's/The Chase/turq/yel	$2.00-4.00
❏ ❏	CJ Sy9805	Pullback Roller: Sylvester & Tweety	$2.00-4.00

CJ Sy9801-05

Checkers

Checkers, as a conglomerate, expanded their acquisitions in the late 1990s to include Carl's Jr., which recently acquired the Hardee's fast food restaurant chain in the Northeast. A fast food chain quite distinctive in appearance, its name is well suited to its black and white checkered tiled restaurants with walk-up and drive-thru windows. The kid's meal program includes a standard hamburger, fries, and a drink, along with the toy.

1990s Checkers restaurant sign

1990s Checkers fast food Restaurant

CK Fairy Tale Classics Kid's Meal, 1998

☐ ☐	Fa9801	Book: *Hansel & Gretal*	$2.00-3.00
☐ ☐	Fa9802	Book: *The Little Mermaid*	$2.00-3.00
☐ ☐	Fa9803	Book: *Princess & the Pea*	$2.00-3.00
☐ ☐	Fa9804	Book: *Gingerbread Boy*	$2.00-3.00
☐ ☐	Fa9805	Book: *Ugly Duckling*	$2.00-3.00
☐ ☐	Fa9806	Book: *Alice & Wonderland*	$2.00-3.00
☐ ☐	Fa9807	Book: *The Three Bears*	$2.00-3.00
☐ ☐	Fa9808	Book: *The Town Mouse & Country Mouse*	$2.00-3.00

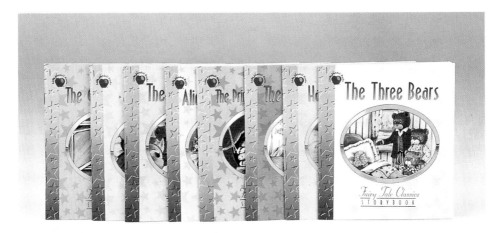

CK Fa9801-08

CK Fa9801-08
translite

CK Jalopies Kid's Meal, 1998

❏ ❏	CH Ja9801	Jalopy Car: red w/ yellow fenders	$2.00-3.00
❏ ❏	CH Ja9802	Jalopy Car: white w/ red fenders	$2.00-3.00
❏ ❏	CH Ja9803	Jalopy Car: black w/ red fenders	$2.00-3.00
❏ ❏	CH Ja9804	Jalopy Car: yellow w/ black fenders	$2.00-3.00

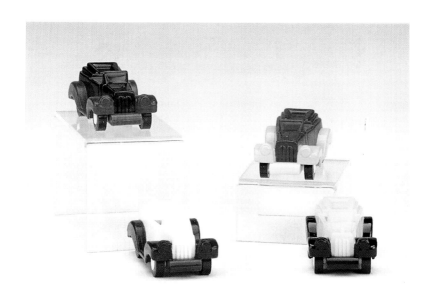

CK Ja9801-04

Chick-fil-A

Chick-fil-A started in 1946 with the S. Truett and Ben Cathy families. They opened a tiny, 24-hour restaurant called the Dwarf Grill, which later became the Dwarf House in the Atlanta suburb of Hapeville. The first restaurant was small: ten counter stools and four tables. By the early 1960s they had developed the taste combination that is now Chick-fil-A's menu; by the 1970s the Truett family moved into mall locations; and by the 1990s they had expanded their operation to reach the $300 million mark in sales. Chick-fil-A is the third largest quick-service chicken restaurant company in the nation.

The "Nugget Meal" is the name of the Chick-fil-A kid's meal promotion; Doodles, a character chicken, is the name of the company's character. Chick-fil-A has restaurant locations in over thirty-one states, with their Chick-fil-A Dwarf House restaurants being the latest design in free-standing restaurants. Located in malls as well as communities, the company's corporate offices are situated in Atlanta, Georgia, where kid's meal premiums are designed to have a moralistic or innovative tone. With each new set of prizes every quarter, Chick-fil-A's Wonderful World approach encourages children to take time and "discover" something new. Chick-fil-A is closed on Sunday to help restaurant employees and patrons maintain life's priorities.

1990s Chick-fil-A sign

Original Home of Chick-fil-A in Hapesville, Georgia

CF On the Go Nugget Meal, 1993

❏ ❏	CF On9301	Train		$2.00-3.00
❏ ❏	CF On9302	Plane		$2.00-3.00
❏ ❏	CF On9303	Helicopter		$2.00-3.00
❏ ❏	CF On9304	Boat		$2.00-3.00
❏ ❏	CF On9305	Truck		$2.00-3.00

CF On9301-05

CF Little Golden Books Nugget Meal, 1994

❏ ❏ CF Li9401	Book: *The Sailor Dog*	$2.00-3.00
❏ ❏ CF Li9402	Book: *The Pokey Little Puppy*	$2.00-3.00
❏ ❏ CF Li9403	Book: *The Saggy Baggy Elephant*	$2.00-3.00
❏ ❏ CF Li9404	Book: *Tawny Scrawny Lion*	$2.00-3.00
❏ ❏ CF Li9405	Book: *The Little Red Caboose*	$2.00-3.00
❏ ❏ CF Li9406	Book: *The Velveteen Rabbit*	$2.00-3.00
❏ ❏ CF Li9407	Book: *The Elves & the Shoemaker*	$2.00-3.00
❏ ❏ CF Li9408	Book: *Little Red Riding Hood*	$2.00-3.00

CF Li9401-08

CF Houses Around the World Viewers, 1996

❏ ❏ CF Ho9601	Africa: grass hut	$2.00-3.00
❏ ❏ CF Ho9602	Australia: sheep station	$2.00-3.00
❏ ❏ CF Ho9603	Asia: Asian house	$2.00-3.00
❏ ❏ CF Ho9604	Antarctica: ice station	$2.00-3.00
❏ ❏ CF Ho9605	Europe: castle	$2.00-3.00
❏ ❏ CF Ho9606	North America: log cabin	$2.00-3.00
❏ ❏ CF Ho9607	South America: adobe hut	$2.00-3.00

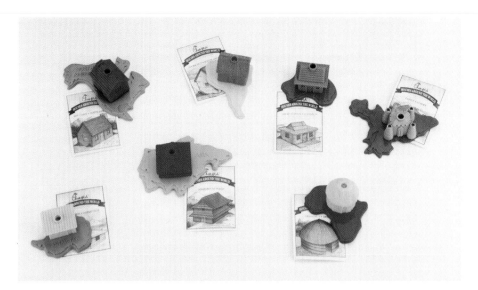

CF Ho9601-07

CF Discover Adventure with Doodles the Explorer Bubble Makers Nugget Meal, 1997

☐ ☐	CF Bu9701	Bubble Blower: Africa/Photo Safari (orange)	$2.00-3.00
☐ ☐	CF Bu9702	Bubble Blower: Antarctica/Admiral (purple)	$2.00-3.00
☐ ☐	CF Bu9703	Bubble Blower: Tyrolean Trekker (red)	$2.00-3.00
☐ ☐	CF Bu9704	Bubble Blower: Australia/Dundee-Outback (lime)	$2.00-3.00
☐ ☐	CF Bu9705	Bubble Blower: Himalayan Mts./Sherpa Guide (blue)	$2.00-3.00
☐ ☐	CF Bu9706	Bubble Blower: West (pink)	$2.00-3.00

CF Bu9701-06

Church's Chicken

Church's Chicken restaurants are primarily located in the South where southern style fried chicken is a regular menu item. They call their kid's meal a "Club House Kid's Meal" and only began giving kid's prizes in the late 1990s. The restaurant characters are named "Churchie Chicken," "Chica Chicken," "Big," and "Juicy-C."

1990s Church's Chicken sign

CC Simpson's Sidewalk Chalk Club House Kid's Meal, 1996

❏ ❏	CC Si9601	Chalk: blue (Marge)	$2.00-3.00
❏ ❏	CC Si9602	Chalk: purple (Homer)	$2.00-3.00
❏ ❏	CC Si9603	Chalk: yellow (Bart)	$2.00-3.00

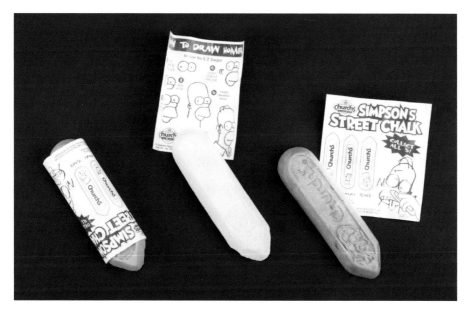

CC Si9601-03

CC Church's Chicken Club House Kid's Meal, 1998

❏ ❏	CC Cc9801	Stuffed Bean Bag: Churchie Chicken	$2.00-3.00
❏ ❏	CC Cc9802	Stuffed Bean Bag: Chica Chicken	$2.00-3.00
❏ ❏	CC Cc9803	Stuffed Bean Bag: Churchie Chicken weight lifting	$2.00-3.00

CC Cc9801-03

Dairy Queen—International Dairy Queen (IDQ)

International Dairy Queen (IDQ) is world renowned for its soft serve ice cream. The company was established in the United States in 1938, near Moline, Illinois, by J. F. Cullough and his son, Alex. The senior McCoullough is often quoted as referring to the cow as "the Queen of the Dairy business." Thus, the Dairy Queen name originated. The very first Dairy Queen store opened in 1940, in Juliet, Illinois.

The Dairy Queen system has evolved over the last fifty-nine years from a few stores in Illinois, selling soft serve ice cream treats, to thousands of stores selling a variety of treats and hot food items. Today there are more than 6,500 franchised Dairy Queen stores in the United States, Canada, Japan, China, the Philippines, Malaysia, Indonesia, Hong Kong, Europe, the Middle East, and Latin America. It is the Dairy Queen Brazier stores, which sell the hot food items, that distribute the myriad of fast food premiums. These Dairy Queen Brazier stores feature hamburgers, hot dogs, various dairy desserts, and other beverages. In addition, Dairy Queen operates approximately 410+ "Orange Julius" stores in malls throughout the United States, plus another 45+ "Karmelkorn" stores featuring popcorn products. Brazier Dairy Queen stores offer different collectible toys at various locations. Stores can choose to distribute from among six national selections a year, with each of these selections having anywhere from four to eight toys. Or they can choose "regional" selections and offer four to twelve or more different toys during the same period. This means that most Brazier Dairy Queen stores are probably offering different toys with their kid's meal promotions all the time, based on ordering quantity and distribution. Over the years, Dairy Queen has successfully used the characters from "Dennis the Menace" to highlight their varied menu selections. The world of Dairy Queen toys is much larger than most collectors have envisioned.

Original Diary Queen roof top figurine

46

1990s Dairy Queen restaurant sign

DQ Prismascopes Kids' Pick-nic Meal, 1991

☐ ☐	DQ Pr9101	Scope: yellow	$2.00-3.00
☐ ☐	DQ Pr9102	Scope: green	$2.00-3.00
☐ ☐	DQ Pr9103	Scope: red	$2.00-3.00
☐ ☐	DQ Pr9104	Scope: blue	$2.00-3.00

DQ Pr9103-04

DQ Rock-A-Doodle Kids' Pick-nic Meal, 1992

❑ ❑	DQ Ro9201	Peepers the Mouse		$3.00-4.00
❑ ❑	DQ Ro9202	Chanticleer the Rooster		$3.00-4.00
❑ ❑	DQ Ro9203	Edmond the Cat		$3.00-4.00
❑ ❑	DQ Ro9204	Patou the Dog		$3.00-4.00
❑ ❑	DQ Ro9205	Grand Duke of Owl		$3.00-4.00
❑ ❑	DQ Ro9206	Snipes the Magpie		$3.00-4.00

DQ Ro9201-06

DQ Holiday Bendies Kids' Pick-nic Meal, 1993

❑ ❑	DQ Ho9301	Santa Awake: *eyes open*		$2.00-3.00
❑ ❑	DQ Ho9302	Santa Asleep: *eyes closed*		$2.00-3.00
❑ ❑	DQ Ho9303	Reindeer w/ green mittens		$2.00-3.00
❑ ❑	DQ Ho9304	Reindeer w/ white mittens		$2.00-3.00

DQ Ho9301-04

DQ Tom & Jerry Kids' Pick-nic Meal, 1993

❏ ❏ DQ To9301 Jerry Sizzling
    Stamper $3.00-4.00
❏ ❏ DQ To9302 Tom Sizzling
    Stamper $3.00-4.00
❏ ❏ DQ To9303 Jerry Squirter
           $3.00-4.00
❏ ❏ DQ To9304 Tom Squirter
           $3.00-4.00
❏ ❏ DQ To9305 Jerry Summer
    Cruiser $3.00-4.00
❏ ❏ DQ To9306 Tom Summer
    Cruiser $3.00-4.00

DQ To9301-06

DQ Alvin & Chipmunks Music Makers Kids' Pick-nic Meal, 1994

❏ ❏	DQ Al9401	Chipmunk's Tambourine	$2.00-3.00
❏ ❏	DQ Al9402	Alvin's Pan Flute	$2.00-3.00
❏ ❏	DQ Al9403	Simon's Maraca	$2.00-3.00
❏ ❏	DQ Al9404	Theodore's Kazoo	$2.00-3.00

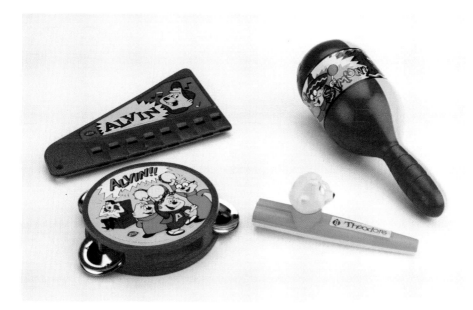

DQ Al9401-04

DQ Dennis the Menace Figurines Kids' Pick-nic Meal, 1994

☐ ☐ DQ Fi9401   Dennis in fire engine $4.00-7.00
☐ ☐ DQ Fi9402   Joey in car $4.00-7.00
☐ ☐ DQ Fi9403   Ruff as dinosaur/3p $4.00-7.00
☐ ☐ DQ Fi9404   Margaret as astronaut/3p $4.00-7.00

DQ Fi9401-04

DQ Bobby's World Kids' Pick-nic Meal, 1995

❑ ❑	DQ Bo9501	Globetrotter	$2.00-3.00
❑ ❑	DQ Bo9502	Bobby's Bulldozer	$2.00-3.00
❑ ❑	DQ Bo9503	Suction Webbly	$2.00-3.00
❑ ❑	DQ Bo9504	Twister Adventure	$2.00-3.00

DQ Bo9501-04

DQ Dennis the Menace Yo-Yo Kids' Pick-nic Meal, 1995

❑ ❑	DQ Yo9501	Yo-Yo: Dennis (blue)	$3.00-5.00
❑ ❑	DQ Yo9502	Yo-Yo: Ruff (orange)	$3.00-5.00

DQ Yo9501-02

DQ The Jetson's Kids' Pick-nic Meal, 1995

❏ ❏ DQ Je9501 Astro's Treadmill
            Workout $2.00-4.00
❏ ❏ DQ Je9502 George & Jane's
            Space Sphere $2.00-4.00
❏ ❏ DQ Je9503 Elroy's Intergalactic
            Twirler $2.00-4.00
❏ ❏ DQ Je9504 Rolling Rosie
                               $2.00-4.00

DQ Je9501-04

DQ Muppet Puppet Cups Kids' Pick-nic Meal, 1995

❏ ❏ DQ Mu9501   Cup: Fozzie w/ Fossie waving fig on brown lid $2.00-3.00
❏ ❏ DQ Mu9502   Cup: Kermit w/ Kermit indicating GOAL on gray lid $2.00-3.00
❏ ❏ DQ Mu9503   Cup: Miss Piggy as cheerleader on purple lid $2.00-3.00
❏ ❏ DQ Mu9504   Cup: Gonzo w/ arms outstretched on yel lid $2.00-3.00

DQ Mu9501-04

DQ Pumpkin Squeeze Balls Kids' Pick-nic Meal, 1995

☐ ☐ DQ Pu9501   Ball: surprised look $2.00-3.00
☐ ☐ DQ Pu9502   Ball: scowling $2.00-3.00
☐ ☐ DQ Pu9503   Ball: laughing $2.00-3.00

DQ Pu9501-03

DQ Bendable Frogs Kids' Pick-nic Meal, 1996

☐ ☐ DQ Fr9601   Yellow Frog $1.00-2.00
☐ ☐ DQ Fr9602   Red Frog $1.00-2.00
☐ ☐ DQ Fr9603   Green Frog $1.00-2.00
☐ ☐ DQ Fr9604   Brown Frog $1.00-2.00

DQ Fr9601-04

DQ Busy World of Richard Scarry Kids' Pick-nic Meal, 1996

❏ ❏	DQ Bu9601	Lowly Worm in red apple car	$3.00-4.00
❏ ❏	DQ Bu9602	Huckle Cat in blue shark car	$3.00-4.00
❏ ❏	DQ Bu9603	Hilda Hippo in purple hippomobile	$3.00-4.00
❏ ❏	DQ Bu9604	Banana Gorilla in yellow banana car	$3.00-4.00

DQ Bu9601-04

DQ Magic School Bus Kids' Pick-nic Meal, 1996

❏ ❏	DQ Ma9601	8-p. Pik-A-Part School Supplies	$2.00-3.00
❏ ❏	DQ Ma9602	Bus Blaster: yellow bus	$2.00-3.00
❏ ❏	DQ Ma9603	5-in-1 Music Maker: blue	$2.00-3.00
❏ ❏	DQ Ma9604	Magic School Bus: yellow	$2.00-3.00

DQ Ma9601-04

DQ National Wild-Life's Kids' Pick-nic Meal, 1996

❏ ❏	DQ Na9601	Europe: Wolverine	$1.00-1.50
❏ ❏	DQ Na9602	North America: Grizzly Bear	$1.00-1.50
❏ ❏	DQ Na9603	Australia: Koala	$1.00-1.50
❏ ❏	DQ Na9604	Africa: Elephant	$1.00-1.50
❏ ❏	DQ Na9605	Asia: Giant Panda	$1.00-1.50
❏ ❏	DQ Na9606	Antarctica: Penguin	$1.00-1.50
❏ ❏	DQ Na9607	South America: Jaguar	$1.00-1.50

DQ Na9601-07

DQ Robot Wind-Up Kids' Pick-nic Meal, 1996

❏ ❏	DQ Ro9601	Blue Robot	$3.00-5.00
❏ ❏	DQ Ro9602	Red Robot	$3.00-5.00

DQ Ro9601-02

DQ Christmas Ornaments Kids' Pick-nic Meal, 1997

❏ ❏	DQ Ch9701	Holiday Wreath (pic frame)	$2.00-3.00
❏ ❏	DQ Ch9702	Home Sweet Dairy Queen (store)	$2.00-3.00
❏ ❏	DQ Ch9703	Ornament Ice Cream Cone	$2.00-3.00
❏ ❏	DQ Ch9704	Winter Time Snowman(pic frame)	$2.00-3.00

DQ Ch9701-04

DQ Dennis the Menace Kids' Pick-nic Meal, 1997

❏ ❏	DQ De9701	Dennis in Soap Box: red launcher	$2.00-4.00
❏ ❏	DQ De9702	Ruff in Wagon: blue launcher	$2.00-4.00
❏ ❏	DQ De9703	Joey in Fire Engine: yellow launcher	$2.00-4.00
❏ ❏	DQ De9704	Margaret w/ Carriage: green launcher	$2.00-4.00
❏ ❏	DQ De9705	Blue Spoon: Dennis	$2.00-4.00
❏ ❏	DQ De9706	Figurine: Dennis	$5.00-8.00
❏ ❏	DQ De9707	Figurine: Margaret	$5.00-8.00

DQ De9701-04

DQ De9706-07

DQ De9705

DQ Felix on the Town Kids' Pick-nic Meal, 1997

☐ ☐	DQ Fe9701	Felix & Mice Dustbin	$2.00-4.00
☐ ☐	DQ Fe9702	First Bank of Felix	$2.00-4.00
☐ ☐	DQ Fe9703	Felix the Cat Mobile	$2.00-4.00
☐ ☐	DQ Fe9704	Felix & Sheba Phone Booth	$2.00-4.00

DQ Fe9701-04

DQ The Flintstones Rock DQ! Kids' Pick-nic Meal, 1997

❏ ❏ DQ Fl9701   Wilma on Keyboard $2.00-4.00
❏ ❏ DQ Fl9702   Fred on Vocals $2.00-4.00
❏ ❏ DQ Fl9703   Dino the Rhythm Ace $2.00-4.00
❏ ❏ DQ Fl9704   Barney on Bongos $2.00-4.00

DQ Fl9701-04

DQ Ocean Stuffed Animals Kids' Pick-nic Meal, 1997

❏ ❏ DQ Oc9701   Frosty Polar Bear $2.00-3.00
❏ ❏ DQ Oc9702   Polly Walrus $2.00-3.00
❏ ❏ DQ Oc9703   Willy Whale $2.00-3.00
❏ ❏ DQ Oc9704   Penny Penguin $2.00-3.00
❏ ❏ DQ Oc9705   Lorenzo Lobster $2.00-3.00

DQ Oc9701-05

DQ Star Trek Deep Space Nine Kids' Pick-nic Meal, 1997

❏ ❏	DQ St9701	U.S.S. Defiant: balancing ship w/ game card	$3.00-5.00
❏ ❏	DQ St9702	Cling-On Sticker Set	$3.00-5.00
❏ ❏	DQ St9703	Space Ball w/ game card	$3.00-5.00
❏ ❏	DQ St9704	Yo-Yo w/ game card	$3.00-5.00

DQ St9701-04

DQ Tiny Tunes Cup Topers Kids' Pick-nic Meal, 1997

❏ ❏	DQ Cu9701	Cup w/ Figurine: Babs Bunny	$2.00-3.00
❏ ❏	DQ Cu9702	Cup w/ Figurine: Dizzy Devil	$2.00-3.00
❏ ❏	DQ Cu9703	Cup w/ Figurine: Buster Bunny	$2.00-3.00
❏ ❏	DQ Cu9704	Cup w/ Figurine: Plucky Duck	$2.00-3.00

DQ Cu9701-04

DQ Dennis the Menace & Friends Rolling Train Kids' Pick-nic Meal, 1998

❑ ❑	DQ Dr9801	Dennis on Purple Engine	$4.00-7.00
❑ ❑	DQ Dr9802	Joey on Red Tanker Car	$4.00-7.00
❑ ❑	DQ Dr9803	Ruff on Yellow Flatcar	$4.00-7.00
❑ ❑	DQ Dr9804	Margaret on Blue Caboose	$4.00-7.00

DQ Dr9801-04

DQ Treats Kids' Pick-nic Meal, 1998

❑ ❑	DQ Tr9801	DQ Mix-n Match Cone	$2.00-4.00
❑ ❑	DQ Tr9802	Banana Split Pullback Racer	$2.00-4.00
❑ ❑	DQ Tr9803	Wind-up Sundae	$2.00-4.00
❑ ❑	DQ Tr9804	Bendable Blizzard	$2.00-4.00
❑ ❑	DQ Tr9805	Rolling DQ Sandwich Water Ball	$2.00-3.00
❑ ❑	DQ Tr9806	Cube	$2.00-3.00

DQ Tr9801-06

Denny's

Created in 1953 from a tiny Danny's Donuts Restaurant in Lakewood, California, the original restaurant sold fresh doughnuts stuffed with jam—not jelly—and high-quality coffee, then a rarity. When a second restaurant was opened in Garden Grove, California, hamburgers, as well as doughnuts, were offered. The chain grew into Denny's, a name chosen by Mr. Harold Butler, the founder. Currently, Denny's is a subsidiary of a Spartanburg, South Carolina, based restaurant group: Advantica Restaurant Group. It currently has 1,600 fully-owned or franchised restaurants nationwide. Their kid's meal program has been sporadic in nature, with The Flintstones and Jetsons themes repeated in

1990s Denny's sign

DE Flintstones Glacier Gliders, 1990

❏ ❏	DE Fl9001	Bam-Bam on Sled: white base	$2.00-3.00
❏ ❏	DE Fl9002	Barney Playing Hockey: blue base	$2.00-3.00
❏ ❏	DE Fl9003	Dino Standing: white base	$2.00-3.00
❏ ❏	DE Fl9004	Fred Ice Skating: blue base	$2.00-3.00
❏ ❏	DE Fl9005	Hoppy on Skis: white base	$2.00-3.00
❏ ❏	DE Fl9006	Pebbles on Snow Disc: white base	$2.00-3.00

DE Fl9001-06

the early years. In the nineties, the kid's meal program—intended for children under 12—was not advertised in many locations and was even discontinued in others. Yearly, rather than monthly, themes are used, such as The Flintstones in 1990 and 1991, and The Jetsons in 1992.

DE Flintstones Vehicles, 1990

☐ ☐	DE Ve9001	Bam-Bam on Tricycle	$2.00-4.00
☐ ☐	DE Ve9002	Barney in a Hollow Tree	$2.00-4.00
☐ ☐	DE Ve9003	Dino in a Wagon	$2.00-4.00
☐ ☐	DE Ve9004	Fred in a Steam Roller	$2.00-4.00
☐ ☐	DE Ve9005	Pebbles in a Plane	$2.00-4.00
☐ ☐	DE Ve9006	Wilma in Race Car	$2.00-4.00

DE Ve9001-06

DE Flintstones Dino-Racers, 1991

☐ ☐	DE Ra9101	Fred on a Tor-Toi-Saurus	$2.00-3.00
☐ ☐	DE Ra9102	Barney on a Purple Dinosaur	$2.00-3.00
☐ ☐	DE Ra9103	Bam-Bam on a Yellow Dinosaur	$2.00-3.00
☐ ☐	DE Ra9104	Betty on a Blue Dinosaur	$2.00-3.00
☐ ☐	DE Ra9105	Dino on a Woolly Mammoth	$2.00-3.00
☐ ☐	DE Ra9106	Pebbles on an Aqua Triceratops	$2.00-3.00

DE Ra9101-06

DE Flintstones Fun Squirters, 1991

❑ ❑ DE Sq9101   Bam-Bam w/ Soda & Ice Cream Cone $2.00-3.00
❑ ❑ DE Sq9102   Barney w/ a Wrist-Sundial $2.00-3.00
❑ ❑ DE Sq9103   Dino w/ Flowers $2.00-3.00
❑ ❑ DE Sq9104   Fred w/ Phone $2.00-3.00
❑ ❑ DE Sq9105   Pebbles w/ Innertube $2.00-3.00
❑ ❑ DE Sq9106   Wilma w/ a Camera $2.00-3.00

DE Sq9101-06

DE The Jetson's Planets, 1992

❑ ❑ DE Pl9201   Planet Ball: Astro/Moon $1.00-2.00
❑ ❑ DE Pl9202   Planet Ball: Elroy/Mars $1.00-2.00
❑ ❑ DE Pl9203   Planet Ball: George/Saturn $1.00-2.00
❑ ❑ DE Pl9204   Planet Ball: Jane/Earth $1.00-2.00
❑ ❑ DE Pl9205   Planet Ball: Judy/Jupiter $1.00-2.00
❑ ❑ DE Pl9206   Planet Ball: Rosie/Neptune $1.00-2.00

DE Pl9201-06

Hardee's

Wilber Hardee started his limited menu fast food restaurant in 1960. The leaves had just begun to turn colors in eastern North Carolina when he ventured into the fast food business. Along with business partners Leonard Rawls Jr. and Jim Gardner, Wilber Hardee named the company Hardee's Drive-Ins, Inc. On Friday, May 5, 1961, the restaurant partners opened their first company-owned, red and white tile Hardee's at Church Street and Falls Road in Rocky Mount, North Carolina. The original menu featured charco-broiled hamburgers (15 cents), cheeseburgers (20 cents), soft drinks (10 cents), and coffee (10 cents). All were served with Hardee's "Jet Service" concept, part of the original ad campaign created for Hardee's. Hardee's enjoyed steady growth throughout the 1960s, operating close to two hundred restaurants near the end of the decade. They acquired Sandy's Systems, an Illinois-based midwest regional chain, and merged the restaurants into Hardee's Systems.

In 1970, Hardee's strengthened its competitive position with a new advertising campaign, "Hurry On Down to Hardee's Where the Burgers are Charco-Broiled," sung by Mama Cass and the New York Jets. The advertising theme was reinforced by characters called Gilbert Giddyup and Speedy McGreedy. Similar to other fast food restaurants, Hardee's introduced the Big Twin hamburger in 1976. By 1978, Hardee's had introduced its Made From Scratch Biscuits, a staple on the menu of several fast food restaurants throughout the 1970s, 1980s, and 1990s.

In the 1980s, Hardee's began its sponsorship association with NASCAR and race car drivers Bobby Allison, Cale Yarborough, and Ward Burton among others. In 1982, Hardee's acquired the Burger Chef chain based in Indianapolis, Indiana. This acquisition led Hardee's management to believe erroneously that they could continue to acquire other fast food restaurants and expand without major problems. By 1983, Hardee's opened their 2,000th restaurant and were on the move to expand worldwide. Early kid's promotions came in "Mealboxes" combining food and purchased premiums. 1987 was the big year for promotions! Hardee's teamed with the California Raisin Advisory Board for a promotion involving the California Raisins, which resulted in the eventual sale of more than fifty million raisin items.

During the 1990s, the height of Hardee's success also saw the demise of Hardee's development of stores. In the early part of the decade, Hardee's bought out the Roy Rogers restaurant chain in an effort to strengthen the company's position in the Northeast. Customers were not happy with the move: Roy Rogers had a loyal following and its customers were not willing to switch to Hardee's.

In response, Hardee's began the Funmeal program for kids, started the Rise and Shine advertising campaign, changed its prime signs from orange and brown to orange and blue, and began a system-wide rollout of Fresh Fried Chicken. They tried everything to increase brand loyalty, but little or nothing seemed to work—the acquisition and merger was just not connecting with the customer base in the Northeast. Hardee's even tried to "Bring Back Roy," but customers did not buy that approach either. They wanted the old Roy Rogers back or nothing. In the end, it was nothing. McDonald's ended up purchasing a large portion of the Hardee's Roy Rogers outlets on the East Coast; Carl's Jr. purchased the remaining company owned units.

As of 1998, Hardee's existed in a very limited number of markets, mainly in the core Carolina market and non-franchised stores. Over-expansion and customer loyalty to other restaurants were two factors leading to the demise of Hardee's broad-based approach. During the company's heyday, their kid's meal was called "Hardee's Funmeal Pack" and the kid's premiums were quality prizes. In the end, Hardee's share of the fast food market was gobbled up by the big kids on the block; what remained of the company-owned Hardee's were bought by Carl's Jr.; and Hardee's kid's meals became known as "Hardee's KIDCO UNDER CONSTRUCTION Funmeal Pack." The regional, privately-owned Hardee's continued to offer quality kid's meal premiums in an effort to win back support for Hardee's and to get the Hardee's ball rolling again.

1990s Hardee's restaurant

HD Days of Thunder Funmeal Pack, 1990

☐ ☐	HD Th9001	City Chevrolet #46 (name on roof)		$2.00-3.00
☐ ☐	HD Th9002	Hardee's #18		$2.00-3.00
☐ ☐	HD Th9003	Mello-Yello #51		$2.00-3.00
☐ ☐	HD Th9004	Superflo #46		$2.00-3.00
☐ ☐	HD Th9005	City Chevrolet #46 (w/o name on roof)		$4.00-6.00

HD Th9001-04

HD Marvel Super Heroes Vehicles Funmeal Pack, 1990

☐ ☐	HD Ma9001	Hulk on Yellow Bulldozer: logo on scoop		$2.00-3.00
☐ ☐	HD Ma9002	Hulk on Yellow Bulldozer: no logo on scoop		$2.00-3.00
☐ ☐	HD Ma9003	She-Hulk in Pink Convertible: logo on hood		$2.00-3.00
☐ ☐	HD Ma9004	She-Hulk in Pink Convertible: no logo on hood		$2.00-3.00
☐ ☐	HD Ma9005	Spiderman on Black Spiderman Car: logo on hood		$2.00-3.00
☐ ☐	HD Ma9006	Spiderman on black Spiderman Car: no logo on hood		$2.00-3.00
☐ ☐	HD Ma9007	Captain America in White Jet Ski: logo on hood		$2.00-3.00
☐ ☐	HD Ma9008	Captain America in White Jet Ski: no logo on hood		$2.00-3.00

HD Ma9002, 03, 05, 07

HD Smurfin' Smurfs Funmeal Pack, 1990

❏ ❏	HD Sm9001	Dog/Blue Skateboard		$2.00-3.00
❏ ❏	HD Sm9002	Smurfette/Green Skateboard		$2.00-3.00
❏ ❏	HD Sm9003	Smurfette/Purple Skateboard		$2.00-3.00
❏ ❏	HD Sm9004	Papa Smurf/Red Skateboard		$2.00-3.00
❏ ❏	HD Sm9005	Smurf/Yellow Skateboard		$2.00-3.00
❏ ❏	HD Sm9006	Smurf on Lunchbox/Orange Skateboard		$2.00-3.00

HD Sm9001-06

HD Squirters Funmeal Pack, 1990

❏ ❏	HD Sq9001	Cheeseburger Squirter		$2.00-3.00
❏ ❏	HD Sq9002	French Fries Squirter		$2.00-3.00
❏ ❏	HD Sq9003	Hot Dog Squirter		$2.00-3.00
❏ ❏	HD Sq9004	Shake Squirter		$2.00-3.00

HD Sq9001-04

HD California Raisins Funmeal Pack, 1991

❏ ❏	HD Ra9101	Anita Break: mother w/ shopping bags	$4.00-8.00
❏ ❏	HD Ra9102	Benny: father w/ bowling ball	$4.00-8.00
❏ ❏	HD Ra9103	Buster: son w/ skateboard	$4.00-8.00
❏ ❏	HD Ra9104	Alotta Stile: daughter w/ radio	$4.00-8.00

HD Ra9101-04

HD Muppet Christmas Carol Finger Puppets Funmeal Pack, 1993

❏ ❏	HD Ch9301	Fp: Fozzie Bear	$1.00-3.00
❏ ❏	HD Ch9302	Fp: Gonzo	$1.00-3.00
❏ ❏	HD Ch9303	Fp: Kermit	$1.00-3.00
❏ ❏	HD Ch9304	Fp: Miss Piggy	$1.00-3.00

HD Ch9301-04

HD Nickelodeon Nicktoon Cruisers Funmeal Pack, 1994

❏ ❏	HD Cr9401	Angelica on Vehicle	$2.00-3.00
❏ ❏	HD Cr9402	Tommy on Vehicle	$2.00-3.00
❏ ❏	HD Cr9403	Porkchop on Vehicle	$2.00-3.00
❏ ❏	HD Cr9404	Doug on Vehicle	$2.00-3.00
❏ ❏	HD Cr9405	Ren on Vehicle	$2.00-3.00
❏ ❏	HD Cr9406	Stimpy on Vehicle	$2.00-3.00
❏ ❏	HD Cr9407	Rocko on Vehicle	$2.00-3.00
❏ ❏	HD Cr9408	Spunky on Vehicle	$2.00-3.00

HD Cr9401-04

HD Cr9405-08

HD Apollo 13 POGS Funmeal Pack, 1995

❏ ❏	HD Ap9501	Milkcaps & Slammer: 6-pack	$1.00-2.00
❏ ❏	HD Ap9502	Blue Slammer	$1.00-2.00
❏ ❏	HD Ap9503	Silver Slammer	$1.00-2.00
❏ ❏	HD Ap9504	Green Slammer	$1.00-2.00

HD Ap9501-04

HD Eek! The Cat Funmeal Pack, 1995

❏ ❏	HD Ee9501	Eek! The Cat: gray cat	$2.00-3.00
❏ ❏	HD Ee9502	Annabelle: pink cat/ribbon in hair	$2.00-3.00
❏ ❏	HD Ee9503	Shark: gray dog/shark	$2.00-3.00
❏ ❏	HD Ee9504	Kutter: star-shaped air toy	$2.00-3.00
❏ ❏	HD Ee9505	Squat: snake air toy	$2.00-3.00
❏ ❏	HD Ee9506	Doc: air toy	$2.00-3.00

HD Ee9501-06

HD X-Men Funmeal Pack, 1995

❑ ❑	HD Xm9501	Tattoo Sheet	$2.00-3.00
❑ ❑	HD Xm9502	Milk Caps (2 strips of 3)	$2.00-3.00
❑ ❑	HD Xm9503	Trading Cards (set of 5)	$2.00-3.00
❑ ❑	HD Xm9504	Mini-Comics 1 & 2	$2.00-3.00
❑ ❑	HD Xm9505	Mini-Comics 3 & 4	$2.00-3.00
❑ ❑	HD Xm9506	Rogue vs. Avalanche Figures	$2.00-4.00
❑ ❑	HD Xm9507	Cyclops vs. Commando Figures	$2.00-4.00
❑ ❑	HD Xm9508	Wolverine vs. The Blob Figures	$2.00-4.00
❑ ❑	HD Xm9509	Phantasia vs. Storm Figures	$2.00-4.00
❑ ❑	HD Xm9610	U-3 Beast Roller Vehicle	$2.00-3.00

HD Xm9506-10

71

HD Holiday Trackers Funmeal Pack, 1996

❏ ❏	HD Sa9601	Santa Claus w/ Santa/candy cane imprint		$2.00-4.00
❏ ❏	HD Sa9602	Sleigh w/ present imprint		$2.00-4.00
❏ ❏	HD Sa9603	Frosty w/ snowman/snowflake imprint		$2.00-4.00
❏ ❏	HD Sa9604	Rudolph w/ reindeer/hoof imprint		$2.00-4.00

HD Sa9601-04

HD Homeward Bound II Funmeal Pack, 1996

❏ ❏	HD Ho9601	Champ: wht dog/brn spots/blk base		$4.00-5.00
❏ ❏	HD Ho9602	Riley: brn sitting dog/grn base		$4.00-5.00
❏ ❏	HD Ho9603	Sassy: cream/brn cat/wht base		$4.00-5.00
❏ ❏	HD Ho9604	Delilah: wht dog/gry base		$4.00-5.00
❏ ❏	HD Ho9605	Shadow: brn standing dog/blue base		$4.00-5.00

HD Ho9601-05

HD Life with Louie Funmeal Pack, 1997

❏ ❏	HD Li9701	The Andersons on a Trike	$2.00-3.00
❏ ❏	HD Li9702	Tommy on His Training Bike	$2.00-3.00
❏ ❏	HD Li9703	Louie on His Sidecar Cycle	$2.00-3.00
❏ ❏	HD Li9704	Louie's Mom & Dad on a Motorcycle	$2.00-3.00

HD Li9701-04

HD Woody Woodpecker Bike Gear Funmeal Pack, 1998

❏ ❏	HD Wo9801	Water Bottle	$2.00-4.00
❏ ❏	HD Wo9802	Wheel Clacker	$2.00-4.00
❏ ❏	HD Wo9803	Bike Spinner	$2.00-4.00
❏ ❏	HD Wo9804	License Plate	$2.00-4.00

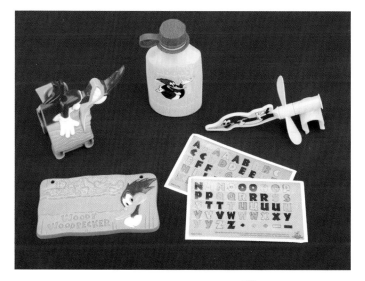

HD Wo9801-04

IHOP

International House of Pancakes (IHOP) is a national chain serving a breakfast, lunch, and dinner menu that revolves around pancakes. Kid's meal premiums are sometimes given to children and sold across the counter to both collectors and children. Over the years, the number of premiums has increased on a smaller scale than at most other fast food restaurants. IHOP's Kid's Meal program, designed for children under the age of twelve, involves an activity placemat menu and a four pack of crayons.

1990s IHOP restaurant sign

IH Pancake Kids Kid's Meal, 1991

❏ ❏	IH Pa9101	Bonnie Blueberry	$2.00-4.00
❏ ❏	IH Pa9102	Chocolate Chip Charlie	$2.00-4.00
❏ ❏	IH Pa9103	Cynthia Cinnamon Apple	$2.00-4.00
❏ ❏	IH Pa9104	Frenchy	$2.00-4.00
❏ ❏	IH Pa9105	Harvey Harvest	$2.00-4.00
❏ ❏	IH Pa9106	Betty Buttermilk: red hair variation	$2.00-4.00
❏ ❏	IH Pa9107	Betty Buttermilk: blond hair variation	$2.00-4.00

IH Pa9101, 03, 04, 07

IH Pancake Kid Cruisers II Kid's Meal, 1993

❏ ❏	IH Pa9301	Cynthia Cinnamon Apple		$3.00-4.00
❏ ❏	IH Pa9302	Von Der Gus		$3.00-4.00
❏ ❏	IH Pa9303	Frenchy		$3.00-4.00
❏ ❏	IH Pa9304	Bonnie Blueberry		$3.00-4.00

IH Pancake Kid Cruisers III Kid's Meal, 1994

❏ ❏	IH Pa9401	Chocolate Chip Charlie		$2.00-4.00
❏ ❏	IH Pa9402	Harvey Harvest		$2.00-4.00
❏ ❏	IH Pa9403	Betty Buttermilk		$2.00-4.00
❏ ❏	IH Pa9404	Susie Strawberry		$2.00-4.00

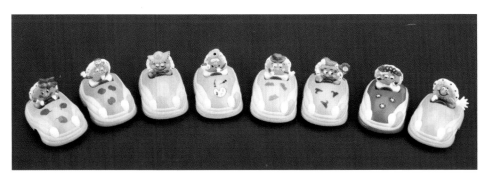

IH Pa9301-04
IH Pa9401-04

IH Kids Can Go! Roller Toys Kid's Meal, 1996

❏ ❏	IH Ki9601	Bonnie Blueberry in Blue Boat	$3.00-5.00
❏ ❏	IH Ki9602	Choc. Chip Charlie on Purple Sktbrd	$3.00-5.00
❏ ❏	IH Ki9603	Susie Strawberry in Pink Jeep	$3.00-5.00
❏ ❏	IH Ki9604	Harvey Harvest in Yellow Plane	$3.00-5.00

IH Ki9601-04

IH Kids Can Go! Roller Toys Kid's Meal, 1997

❏ ❏	IH Ro9701	Frenchy on Purple Motorcycle	$3.00-4.00
❏ ❏	IH Ro9702	Von Der Gus in Blue IHOP Truck	$2.00-4.00
❏ ❏	IH Ro9703	Rosanna Banana Nut in Green Car	$2.00-4.00
❏ ❏	IH Ro9704	Cynthia Cinnamon Apple in Fire Engine	$2.00-4.00

IH Ro9701-04

Jack in the Box

In 1951, the Jack in the Box restaurant chain was founded by Robert O. Peterson of San Diego, who wanted to attract children to his series of restaurants. Headquartered in San Diego, the Jack in the Box organization currently operates and franchises more than 1,300 Jack in the Box restaurants in twelve states. An oversized version of the children's toy clown popping out of a box was originally installed as a restaurant attraction, with the expectation that a toy popping quickly out of a box would translate into getting your *food* fast. In the 1950s, a Jack in the Box hamburger sold for 29 cents and the Hot Apple Turnover sold for 17 cents. At that time, Jack in the Box restaurants were located primarily in California, Texas, and Arizona. They featured a smiling clown named Jack who greeted motorists ordering through a two-way speaker device inside Jack's head.

Jack Bendables, a collectible premium, was first introduced in the early 1960s. Also in the '60s, acquisition of the chain by Foodmarker, Inc. led to a gradual change in menu selection; the menu was primarily tailored to adult taste during the 1970s. Jack Bendables were reintroduced in the 1970s, remolded, and sold for 99 cents.

In a 1980s television ad, the company blew up Jack, the clown icon who once served as the company's speakerbox at the drive-thrus. This was to signal the company's market re-positioning to totally adult tastes and upscale menu choices. By 1995, however, Jack was reintroduced as the company founder in a new "Jack's Back" advertising and marketing campaign. The ads featured Jack as a model corporate executive in the nineties. Designed to build a powerful brand image for Jack in the Box products, the ad campaign helped to promote innovative new products for adults and children alike. Since Jack returned in 1996, he has been transformed from a clown

1990s Jack in the Box sign

into a witty, irreverent CEO and founder of the Jack in the Box fast food hamburger chain.

In 1997, Jack's Vehicle promotions became a timely sequel to the more than two million Jack Antenna Toppers distributed, the more than one million Bendable Jack figures distributed, and the more than one hundred thousand Jack Holiday Ornaments sold since the "Jack's Back" ad campaign began. The Antenna Toppers were 3-D white balls with Jack's trademark yellow hat, blue eyes, black nose, and a wide, red smile. They sold for 99 cents each at most restaurants and were created in the image of Jack, the chain's founder. The original cast of Jack in the Box characters were Jack, Clownie, the Swiss Yodeler, Onion Ring, and Spy, which has been expanded over the years to include Jumbo Jack, Sly Fry, Betty Burger, Edgar E. Eggroll, and Ollie O. Ring. All of these characters are called "The Jack Pack." "Jack" premiums continue to be very sought after by collectors, and since Jack's promotions are neither national nor regional in scope, different ones can be found at different restaurants in the same town at the same time.

JB Jack in the Box Bendables Kid's Meal, 1990

❏	❏	JB Be9001	Ollie O. Ring	$7.00-10.00
❏	❏	JB Be9002	Sly Fry	$7.00-10.00
❏	❏	JB Be9003	Edgar E. Eggroll	$7.00-10.00
❏	❏	JB Be9004	Jumbo Jack	$7.00-10.00
❏	❏	JB Be9005	Betty Burger	$7.00-10.00

JB Be9002-5

JB Jack in the Box Bendables Kid's Meal, 1991

❏ ❏ JB Be9101   Ollie O. Ring: purple ring $7.00-10.00
❏ ❏ JB Be9102   Sly Fry: red $7.00-10.00
❏ ❏ JB Be9103   Edgar E. Eggroll: light blue $7.00-10.00
❏ ❏ JB Be9104   Jumbo Jack: red $7.00-10.00
❏ ❏ JB Be9105   Betty Burger: pink $7.00-10.00

JB Be9101-5

JB Finger Puppets Kid's Meal, 1992

❏ ❏ JB Fi9201   Fp: Betty Burger w/ white gloves $7.00-10.00
❏ ❏ JB Fi9202   Fp: Edgar E. Eggroll w/ red bow tie $7.00-10.00
❏ ❏ JB Fi9203   Fp: Jumbo Jack w/ blue glasses/red lenses $7.00-10.00
❏ ❏ JB Fi9204   Fp: Ollie O. Ring w/ white gloves $7.00-10.00
❏ ❏ JB Fi9205   Fp: Sly Fry w/ red frames $7.00-10.00

JB Fi9201-05

JB Jack's Holiday Ornament Kid's Meal, 1995

❑ ❑ JB Ho9501   Jack Ornament: snowman
$4.00-5.00

JB Star Trek Generations Kid's Meal, 1995

❑ ❑ JB St9501   Milkcaps: 3 Villains
$3.00-4.00
❑ ❑ JB St9502   Milkcaps: Data + 2
$3.00-4.00
❑ ❑ JB St9503   Milkcaps: 3 Spaceships
$3.00-4.00
❑ ❑ JB St9504   Milkcaps: Pickard + 2
$3.00-4.00
❑ ❑ JB St9505   Tattoo Sticker Sheet
$2.00-3.00
❑ ❑ JB St9506   Static Movie Poster
$2.00-4.00

JB Ho9501

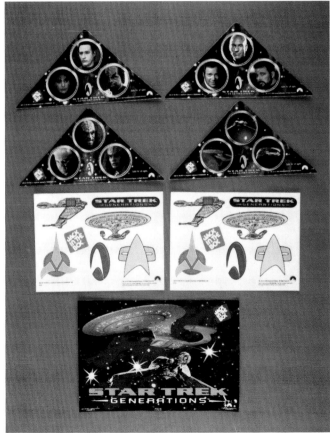

JB St9501-06

JB Doug Kid's Meal, 1996

❑ ❑	JB Do9601	Porkchop: dog		$2.00-5.00
❑ ❑	JB Do9602	Patti w/ Crown Skeeter & Helmet		$2.00-5.00
❑ ❑	JB Do9603	Roger w/ Dracula Cape		$2.00-5.00
❑ ❑	JB Do9604	Judy w/ Matador Outfit		$2.00-5.00
❑ ❑	JB Do9605	Doug w/ "Q" on Shirt		$2.00-5.00
❑ ❑	JB Do9606	Skeeter w/ "Light Bolt" on Shirt		$2.00-5.00

JB Do9601-06

JB Jack's Back Kid's Meal, 1996

❑ ❑	JB Ja9601	Jack in Black Suit w/ Hamburger		$5.00-8.00
❑ ❑	JB Ja9602	Jack in Blue Suit w/ Brief Case		$5.00-8.00
❑ ❑	JB Ja9603	Jack in Gray Suit w/ Cellular Phone		$5.00-8.00

JB Ja9601-03

JB Extreme Machines Kid's Meal, 1997

❏ ❏ JB Ex9701   Red Plane $1.00-2.00
❏ ❏ JB Ex9702   Blue Plane $1.00-2.00
❏ ❏ JB Ex9703   Green Dragster $1.00-2.00
❏ ❏ JB Ex9704   Yellow Dragster $1.00-2.00
❏ ❏ JB Ex9705   Red Pick-Up $1.00-2.00
❏ ❏ JB Ex9706   Purple Pick-Up $1.00-2.00
❏ ❏ JB Ex9707   U-3 Sticker Sheet $1.00-2.00

JB Ex9701-06

JB Holiday Kid's Meal, 1997

❏ ❏ JB Ho9701 Snowman's Face $2.00-4.00

JB Ho9701

JB Bendable Jack Figures Kid's Meal, 1998

❏ ❏	JB Be9801	Jack w/ Newspaper		$4.00-5.00
❏ ❏	JB Be9802	Jack w/ Computer		$4.00-5.00
❏ ❏	JB Be9803	Jack w/ Hamburger		$4.00-5.00
❏ ❏	JB Be9804	Jack w/ Golf Club		$4.00-5.00

JB Be9801-04

JB Jack's Vehicles Kid's Meal, 1998

❏ ❏	JB Ve9801	Jack in Helicopter: black		$3.00-4.00
❏ ❏	JB Ve9802	Jack on Motorcycle: purple		$3.00-4.00
❏ ❏	JB Ve9803	Jack in a GTO Car: red		$3.00-4.00
❏ ❏	JB Ve9804	Jack on Tractor: yellow		$3.00-4.00
❏ ❏	JB Ve9805	Jack in Golf Cart: turquoise		$3.00-4.00
❏ ❏	JB Ve9806	U-3 Red Volkswagon		$3.00-5.00

JB Ve9801-06

KFC

In 1939 in Corbin, Kentucky, Colonel Harland D. Sanders, a jolly looking man with a white beard, perfected a secret blend of eleven herbs and spices. When Colonel Sanders decided to enter the restaurant business in 1952, Pete Harman of Salt Lake City, Utah, became the first Kentucky Fried Chicken (KFC) franchise owner. The restaurants were incorporated into the Kentucky Fried Chicken Corporation by 1955, but success and the accelerated pace of the fast food business led the Colonel to sell out to a group of investors in 1964. After all, the Colonel was not a young man.

By 1970, the franchise was listed on the New York Stock Exchange and Colonel Sanders bought the first one hundred shares. When Kentucky Fried Chicken was bought out by Heublein, Inc. in 1971, the Colonel became unhappy with the direction the company was taking and threatened to re-enter the fast food restaurant business if his ideas on quality products were not used. Colonel Sanders died in 1980, but the KFC corporation listened to and implemented many of his ideas for improvement, even though the Colonel did not live long enough to see most of them achieve fruition.

In the 1980s, KFC became a subsidiary of R. J. Reynolds Industries, which subsequently became RJR Nabisco, Inc. Expanding, contracting, and changing ownership in the 1980s led KFC to open their 5,000th restaurant in 1989.

By the 1990s, KFC had introduced a new logo to emphasize the variety of its chicken products: in addition to fried chicken, KFC now offered chicken pot pies and several variations of baked and grilled chicken products. The lure of the diet-conscious consumer dollar was forcing a change in the company's image as well, and, by 1993, all KFC restaurants offered non-fried chicken items as part of their menu selections. In 1994, the company began testing kid's meal promotional toys, at first tied to the Looney Tunes characters. A year later, the KFC Kids Meal program was begun, continuing successfully throughout the nineties and maintaining use of the Colonel's image as a means of attracting consumer dollars.

1990s KFC restaurant

KF Matchbox Cars Kids Meal, 1995

❑ ❑	KF Ma9501	Orange/White Ambulance	$2.00-4.00
❑ ❑	KF Ma9502	Snorkel Fire Engine	$2.00-4.00
❑ ❑	KF Ma9503	Orange/Black Mustang	$2.00-4.00
❑ ❑	KF Ma9504	Orange Jeep 4x4	$2.00-4.00
❑ ❑	KF Ma9505	Purple Ferrari 456 GT	$2.00-4.00
❑ ❑	KF Ma9506	Red BMW 850	$2.00-4.00

KF Ma9501-05

KF Garfield 500 Kids Meal, 1996

❏ ❏ KF Ga9601   Grand Prix Garfield $2.00-4.00
❏ ❏ KF Ga9602   Off-Road Odie $2.00-4.00
❏ ❏ KF Ga9603   Chug-A-Long Nermal $2.00-4.00
❏ ❏ KF Ga9604   Cruisin' Jon $2.00-4.00
❏ ❏ KF Ga9605   Warp Speed Pooky $2.00-4.00
❏ ❏ KF Ga9606   Airborne Arlene $2.00-4.00

KF Ga9601-05

KF Marvel Super Heroes Kids Meal, 1997

❏ ❏ KF Su9701   Spider-Man Wall Walker $2.00-3.00
❏ ❏ KF Su9702   Spider-Man Symbol Clip $2.00-3.00
❏ ❏ KF Su9703   Invisible Woman Escape Launcher $2.00-3.00
❏ ❏ KF Su9704   Incredible Hulk Pencil Twirler $2.00-3.00
❏ ❏ KF Su9705   Fantastic Four Terra Craft $2.00-3.00
❏ ❏ KF Su9706   Wolverine Press 'n Go $2.00-3.00

KF Su9701-06

KF Beakman's World Kids Meal, 1998

❏ ❏	KF Be9801	Dancing Liza: Magnetism	$2.00-3.00
❏ ❏	KF Be9802	Beakman's Balancer: Gravity	$2.00-3.00
❏ ❏	KF Be9803	Diver Don: Propulsion	$2.00-3.00
❏ ❏	KF Be9804	Lester Reverser: Stored Energy	$2.00-3.00
❏ ❏	KF Be9805	Optical Illusion Top	$2.00-3.00
❏ ❏	KF Be9806	Penguin TV: Optical Illusion	$2.00-3.00

KF Be9801-06

KF Wallace & Gromit Kids Meal, 1998

❏ ❏	KF Sp9801	The Wrong Trousers: Wallace fig/wht t-shirt/grn shorts/plastic	$2.00-3.00
❏ ❏	KF Sp9802	Gromit's Roll-along Sidecar: Wallace/Gromit in red airplane	$2.00-3.00
❏ ❏	KF Sp9803	Blinking Feathers McGraw: Penguin fig pink feet/orange peak	$2.00-3.00
❏ ❏	KF Sp9804	Sheep-on-a-String: Gromit fig on string black/white w/ extended body	$2.00-3.00
❏ ❏	KF Sp9805	U-3 Wallace & Gromit Character Card Set: Wallace/Gromit Cards/1 card/3-D style + 4 cards	$2.00-3.00
❏ ❏	KF Sp9806	U-3 Wallace Bendable: Wallace fig brn pants/grn shirt bendable	$2.00-3.00

KF Sp9801-06

K-Mart

K-Mart Corporation is one of the nation's largest discount retailers and one of the world's largest mass merchandise retailers. K-Mart operates older, traditional discount stores and modernistic Super K-Mart centers in all fifty of the United States. Based in Troy, Michigan, K-Mart began a limited menu kid's program in the mid-nineties. The few promotions offered can last for months, even years in some cases.

K-Mart initially called their few promotions "K-Mart Kids' Meal, Where Food is Fun" and later in the 1990s, Super K launched themselves into the promotional giveaway race to attract consumer dollars. In late 1997, K-Mart began calling their kid's meal program "K-Mart Kid'Addle Kids' Meal" and Super K called their program "K Cafe Kids Combo Meal."

1990s K-Mart sign

KM Frisbee Flyers Kids' Meals, 1994

❏ ❏	KM Fr9401	Frisbee: orange	$1.00-1.50
❏ ❏	KM Fr9402	Frisbee: yellow	$1.00-1.50
❏ ❏	KM Fr9403	Frisbee: green	$1.00-1.50

KM Fr9401-03

KM Leaky Tiki Totems Kids' Meals, 1995

❏ ❏ KM To9501   Totem: Loony Lagoony (red) $2.00-2.50
❏ ❏ KM To9502   Totem: Golly Wally (yellow) $2.00-2.50
❏ ❏ KM To9503   Totem: Silly Spilly (green) $2.00-2.50

KM To9501-03

KM Disney's Toy Story Kid'Addle Kids' Meal, 1997

❏ ❏ KM To9701   Toy Story Sliding Puzzle: Alien $2.00-3.00
❏ ❏ KM To9702   Toy Story Sliding Puzzle: Buzz Lightyear $2.00-3.00
❏ ❏ KM To9703   Toy Story Sliding Puzzle: Woody $2.00-3.00
❏ ❏ KM To9704   Toy Story Sliding Puzzle: Bo Peep $2.00-3.00
❏ ❏ KM To9705   Toy Story Sliding Puzzle: Hamm $2.00-3.00

KM To9701-05

Long John Silver' s

Jerrico (a conglomerate company) owned Fazoli's Restaurants in 1989. By 1990, they were bought out in a leveraged buyout and the name was changed to Long John Silver's Restaurants Inc. Fazoli's original five stores were sold off and the short-lived history of Long John Silver's began. During the 1990s, Long John Silver's became a nationally franchised chain of restaurants offering fast food seafood variety meals to kids. Focusing on "Fun & Fish" meals for kids, Long John Silver's started their kid's meal in the 1980s with a box called the treasure chest and continued into the late 1990s with a variety of kid's meal bags and products.

Long John Silver's characters in their Undersea Adventures include: Captain Flint, The Parrot; Long John Silver, The Buccaneer; Billy Bones, The Pirate; and Ophelia Octopus, The Sidekick. Their kid's meal is typically called Long John Silver's Fish & Fun Kid's Meal. In late June 1998, however, Long John Silver's filed for bankruptcy protection from creditors and closed 70 of its nearly 1,400 stores, a decline that continued on a monthly basis. The fast food market for kid's fish related meals is fiercely competitive, and Long John Silver' s is a victim of the profit decline in all fast food establishments. The "sizzle" was just not evident in the Fish & Fun Kid's Meal program—the premiums were interesting, but not exciting enough to attract the kids and get them hooked on fish. Essentially, Long John Silver's lost the "bait" that could have caught the gold when Fazoli's was sold off.

1990s Long John Silver' s restaurant

LJ Sea Walkers Fish & Fun Kid's Meal, 1990

❏ ❏ LJ Se9001   Walker: Captain Flint, the Parrot $7.00-10.00
❏ ❏ LJ Se9002   Walker: Quinn, the Penguin $7.00-10.00
❏ ❏ LJ Se9003   Walker: Sydney, Yellow Sea Monster $7.00-10.00
❏ ❏ LJ Se9004   Walker: Sylvia, Purple Sea Monster $7.00-10.00
❏ ❏ LJ Se9005   Walker: Flash, the Turtle $7.00-10.00

LJ Se9001-04

LJ Water Blasters Sea Squirters Fish & Fun Kid's Meal, 1990

❏ ❏ LJ Sq9001   Squirter: Long John Silver w/ blue hat $3.00-5.00
❏ ❏ LJ Sq9002   Squirter: Ophelia Octopus/blue w/ grn hands $3.00-5.00
❏ ❏ LJ Sq9003   Squirter: Billy Bob w/ red kerchief $3.00-5.00
❏ ❏ LJ Sq9004   Squirter: Captain Flint/parrot $3.00-5.00

LJ Sq9001-04

LJ Free Willy 2 Fish & Fun Kid's Meal, 1995

❏ ❏	LJ Fr9501	Boy: Jesse	$2.00-3.00
❏ ❏	LJ Fr9502	Whale: Little Spot	$2.00-2.00
❏ ❏	LJ Fr9503	Whale: Willy	$2.00-2.00
❏ ❏	LJ Fr9504	Whale: Luna	$2.00-2.00

LJ Fr9501-04

LJ Monster Wrestlers In My Pocket Fish & Fun Kid's Meal, 1996

❏ ❏	LJ Mo9601	Wrestler: Sarge (blue)	$2.00-3.00
❏ ❏	LJ Mo9602	Wrestler: Stomper (red)	$2.00-3.00
❏ ❏	LJ Mo9603	Wrestler: Bullday (white)	$2.00-3.00
❏ ❏	LJ Mo9604	Wrestler: Gargoyle (purple)	$2.00-3.00
❏ ❏	LJ Mo9605	Wrestler: Grunt (black)	$2.00-3.00
❏ ❏	LJ Mo9606	Wrestler: Goonie (turquoise)	$2.00-3.00

LJ Mo9601-06

LJ Pound Puppies Fish & Fun Kid's Meal, 1996

❏ ❏	LJ Po9601	Dalmation	$2.00-3.00
❏ ❏	LJ Po9602	Tan Laying on Back	$2.00-3.00
❏ ❏	LJ Po9603	Tan Sitting	$2.00-3.00
❏ ❏	LJ Po9604	Brown Sitting Up	$2.00-3.00
❏ ❏	LJ Po9605	Beige Laying Down	$2.00-3.00
❏ ❏	LJ Po9606	Gray Laying on Back	$2.00-3.00
❏ ❏	LJ Po9607	White Laying Down	$2.00-3.00
❏ ❏	LJ Po9608	White/Tan Ears Sitting Up	$2.00-3.00

LJ Po9601-08

LJ Disney Straw Huggers Fish & Fun Kid's Meal, 1997

❏ ❏	LJ Di9701	Straw Hugger: Goofy	$2.00-4.00
❏ ❏	LJ Di9702	Straw Hugger: Dale	$2.00-4.00
❏ ❏	LJ Di9703	Straw Hugger: Scrooge McDuck	$2.00-4.00
❏ ❏	LJ Di9704	Straw Hugger: Baloo	$2.00-4.00

LJ Di9701-04

LJ Joe Cool Peanuts Explorer Secret Agent Fish & Fun Kid's Meal, 1997

❑ ❑	LJ Jo9701	Squirter/Camera	$3.00-5.00
❑ ❑	LJ Jo9702	Flute/Pen/Whistle	$3.00-5.00
❑ ❑	LJ Jo9703	Flashlight/Telescope	$3.00-5.00
❑ ❑	LJ Jo9704	Wrist Watch/Magnifier	$3.00-5.00

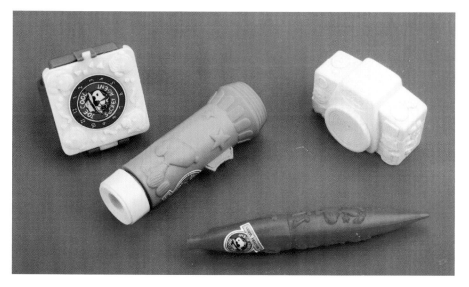

LJ Jo9701-04

LJ Lost in Space Fish & Fun Kid's Meal, 1998

❏ ❏	LJ Lo9801	Pilot Don West	$2.00-4.00
❏ ❏	LJ Lo9802	Blawp	$2.00-4.00
❏ ❏	LJ Lo9803	Robot	$2.00-4.00
❏ ❏	LJ Lo9804	Future Smith	$2.00-4.00

LJ Lo9801-04

Nathan's

Located along the interstate highways at rest stops and within airport concourses, Nathan's serves primarily hot dogs. It has developed a marketing segment for the all-American hot dog and associated spin-off products, like popcorn and sodas. They offer kid's meal toys at only a select number of stores, which makes collecting Nathan's premiums a challenge.

1990s Nathan's restaurant

NA Franksters Kid's Meal, 1998

☐ ☐	NA Fr9801	Hot Dog Figure: Clown Outfit	$4.00-5.00
☐ ☐	NA Fr9802	Hot Dog Figure: Ring Master Outfit	$4.00-5.00
☐ ☐	NA Fr9803	Hot Dog Figure: Lion Tamer's Outfit	$4.00-5.00
☐ ☐	NA Fr9804	Hot Dog Figure: Female Trapeze Artist Outfit	$4.00-5.00

Na Fr9801-04

Pizza Hut

Pizza Hut began in Wichita, Kansas, in 1958. The red roof design was adopted by 1969—and Pizza Hut was on a roll. By 1974, they had 1,400 units and by 1982 ET promotion gave magic to dining-in. In 1984, the famous BOOK-IT program for children was started. An Honor Roll report card earned a *free* Personal Pan pizza to the hard-working child. Three years later, The Flintstones glasses were promoted and in 1998 Pizza Hut celebrated their Thirtieth Anniversary.

Pizza Hut was owned by PepsiCo, Inc. until January 1997, when it was spun off to PepsiCo shareholders as an independent, publicly-traded company named Tricon Corporation. This corporation owns Pizza Hut, Taco Bell, and KFC. Tricon is closing the non-profitable Pizza Huts, mainly those originally designed as eat-in establishments, and revising their Pizza Hut Munch Down Meal program. Like going to a drive-in movie, going out to eat pizza has fallen out of vogue with adult consumers of the 1990s.

Initially, Pizza Hut's kid's meal program was designed to incorporate the eat-in, sit down drink cup along with the toy promotion to add a little extra "zip" to the pizza meal. Changing from sit down meals to carry-out all but eliminated the need for a specialized drink cup. The toy premium offering has continued throughout the nineties, although sporadically at times.

In the early 1990s, premiums such as Eureeka's Castle large character hand puppets were sold over the counter as self-liquidators. By the mid 1990s, a typical promotion included a specially designed pizza box (medium and large size), placemat for any dine-in customer, specially designed cup (medium and large), and a premium toy (given and/or sold across the counter). When an U-3 (under 3) child was present, crayons and a menu with a sticker sheet were provided. The only hitch was that promotional toys were not always available; nor were fill-ins regularly available, which led to disappointment by dine-in children and to frustration with the company. On a yearly basis, Pizza Hut does about a half dozen promotions. In the past, it has more like "Pot Luck Dinner at Pizza Hut" when it came to promotional kid's meal toys.

1990s Pizza Hut restaurant sign

1990s Pizza Hut restaurant

PH Fievel Goes West Munch Down Meal, 1991

❏ ❏ PH Fi9101	Cup: Cat R. Waul w/ red top hat	$5.00-8.00
❏ ❏ PH Fi9102	Cup: Fievel w/ gray ten gallon hat	$5.00-8.00
❏ ❏ PH Fi9103	Cup: Wylie Burp w/ tan, high brim hat	$5.00-8.00

PH Fi9101-03

PH Beauty & the Beast Munch Down Meal, 1992

❏ ❏ PH Be9201	Puzzle: Lumiere/Be Our Guest Dance	$4.00-5.00
❏ ❏ PH Be9202	Puzzle: Mrs. Potts, Lumiere, & Cogsworth	$4.00-5.00
❏ ❏ PH Be9203	Puzzle: Beauty & the Beast/dance scene	$4.00-5.00

PH Be9201

PH X-Men Comics & Videos Munch Down Meal, 1993

❏ ❏ PH Xm9301   Comic: #1 Clash w/ Sentinels $2.00-4.00
❏ ❏ PH Xm9302   Comic: #2 Skyjacked $2.00-4.00

PH Xm9301-02

PH Air Extremes Munch Down Meal, 1994

❏ ❏ PH Ai9401   Gyro-Copter $3.00-5.00
❏ ❏ PH Ai9402   Power Glider $3.00-5.00
❏ ❏ PH Ai9403   Stunt Plane $3.00-5.00
❏ ❏ PH Ai9404   Windmill $3.00-5.00
❏ ❏ PH Ai9405   U-3 Activity Booklet $2.00-3.00

PH Ai9401-04

PH Marsupilami Houba Douba! Munch Down Meal, 1994

❏ ❏	PH Ma9401	Glow Ball (clear)	$2.00-2.50
❏ ❏	PH Ma9402	Marsupilami Jump Rope (yellow)	$2.00-3.00
❏ ❏	PH Ma9403	Marsupilami Yo-Yo (yellow/purple)	$3.00-4.00

PH Ma9401-03

PH Flipper Munch Down Meal, 1996

❏ ❏	PH Fl9601	Flipper w/ Scar the Shark on purple stand	$2.00-4.00
❏ ❏	PH Fl9602	Flipper Wave Rider on pink stand	$2.00-4.00
❏ ❏	PH Fl9603	Flipper Balancing Trick on red ring	$2.00-4.00

PH Fl9601-03

Popeyes

Popeyes fast food restaurants began their Kid's Meal program in late 1998 with dinosaur figures. Prior to the late 1990s, Popeyes gave out a series of four rubber character figurines. During 1999 Popeyes began a series of specially designed kid's meal bags and premiums promoting the meal with the name of "Voyager Meal."

Popeyes Voyager Meal Bag

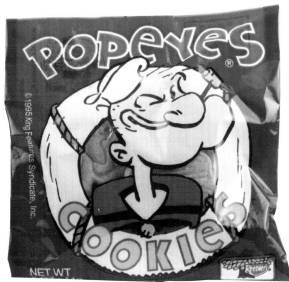

Popeyes Kids Meal Cookies

105

PO Character Figurines, 1990

❏ ❏	PO Ch9001	Popeye Holding a Can of Spinach	$3.00-5.00
❏ ❏	PO Ch9002	Bluto Wearing a Hat	$3.00-5.00
❏ ❏	PO Ch9003	Sweet Pea	$3.00-5.00
❏ ❏	PO Ch9004	Popeye Holding a Pipe	$3.00-5.00

PO Ch9001-04

PO Dino Figurines Voyager Meal, 1998

❏ ❏ PO Di9801 Dinosaurs: 12 dif. species $2.00-4.00 ea.

PO Di9801-09

PO Silhouette Super Balls Voyager Meal, 1998

☐ ☐	PO Su9801	Super Ball Popeye: blue, red, grn, or org	$3.00-4.00
☐ ☐	PO Su9802	Super Ball Olive Oly: blue, red, grn, or org	$3.00-4.00
☐ ☐	PO Su9803	Super Ball Bluto: blue, red, grn, or org	$3.00-4.00
☐ ☐	PO Su9804	Super Ball Sweet Pea: blue, red, grn, or org	$3.00-4.00

PO Su9801-04

PO Space Travel Jigsaw Puzzles, 1999

☐ ☐	PO Sp9901	Puzzle: Astronaut w/ Lunar Lander & US flag	$3.00-5.00
☐ ☐	PO Sp9902	Puzzle: Space Shuttle Launch	$3.00-5.00
☐ ☐	PO Sp9903	Puzzle: Earth view	$3.00-5.00
☐ ☐	PO Sp9904	Puzzle: Saturn & planets	$3.00-5.00

PO Sp9901 box

PO Sp9901 puzzle

PO Sp9902 Puzzle: Space Shuttle Launch and PO Sp9904 Puzzle: Saturn & planets

PO Sp9901 Puzzle: Astronaut w/ Lunar Lander & US flag and PO Sp9903 Puzzle: Earth view

Roy Rogers

Roy Rogers restaurants were born in the 1960s in Cincinnati, Ohio, home of Frisch's Big Boy restaurant chain. In an expansion move, the owners of Frisch's decided to open another chain of restaurants and call them Roy Rogers. These restaurants were designed to offer roast beef sandwiches and appeal to the hardy, western style market of consumers looking for an alternative to hamburgers.

Roy Rogers's approach to kid's meals premiums was to put the toy in a capsule under the drink cup. This was a novel idea, except for the fact that it limited the size of the prize. The 1980s and early 1990s were the heydays for Roy Rogers: their kid's meals came in very decorative bags and the prizes were innovative. By 1996, the chain was sold to the Marriott Corporation, which in turn sold it to Hardee's, which in turn sold segments of the stores to McDonald's. By 1996, Roy Rogers was all but "Adios, Amigo" in many markets, especially on the East Coast. Many factors led to the demise of Roy Rogers, the greatest of which was Hardee's ill-fated timing in attempting to replace Roy Rogers fast food with that of Hardee's. Customers did not buy the switch. The "Bring Back Roy's" campaign ultimately turned into the "End of the Trail," with Roy Rogers fast food restaurants fading into the sunset.

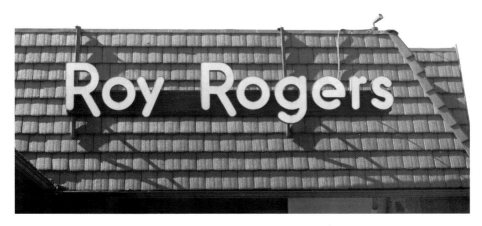

1990s Roy Rogers restaurant sign

1990s Roy Rogers generic kid's
meal premium

RR Critters Meal, 1990

☐ ☐	RR Cr9001	Critter w/ blue eyes	$2.00-3.00
☐ ☐	RR Cr9002	Critter w/ red eyes	$2.00-3.00
☐ ☐	RR Cr9003	Critter w/ white eyes	$2.00-3.00
☐ ☐	RR Cr9004	Critter w/ yellow eyes	$2.00-3.00

RR Cr9001-04

RR Star Searchers Meal, 1990

☐ ☐	RR St9001	Circle Saucer Space Vehicle	$2.00-4.00
☐ ☐	RR St9002	Space Shuttle Space Vehicle: grn/purple shuttle	$2.00-4.00
☐ ☐	RR St9003	Lunar Robot Space Vehicle: grn/purple	$2.00-4.00
☐ ☐	RR St9004	Lunar Rover Space Vehicle	$2.00-4.00

RR St9001-03

RR Animal Meal, 1992

☐ ☐ RR An9201   Team Helmets: 28 dif. teams
$2.00-3.00 ea.

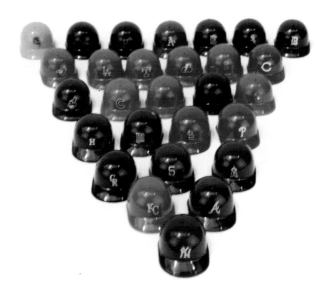

RR An9201

RR Cup Critters Meal, 1994

- ❑ ❑ RR Cu9401 Cup Critter: Frog
  $2.00-3.00
- ❑ ❑ RR Cu9402 Cup Critter: Lion
  $2.00-3.00
- ❑ ❑ RR Cu9403 Cup Critter: Pig
  $2.00-3.00
- ❑ ❑ RR Cu9404 Cup Critter:
  Beaver $2.00-3.00
- ❑ ❑ RR Cu9405 Cup Critter: Bear
  $2.00-3.00
- ❑ ❑ RR Cu9406 Cup Critter: Duck
  $2.00-3.00
- ❑ ❑ RR Cu9407 Cup Critter:
  Elephant $2.00-3.00
- ❑ ❑ RR Cu9408 Cup Critter: Turtle
  $2.00-3.00
- ❑ ❑ RR Cu9409 Cup Critter:
  Alligator $2.00-3.00

RR Cu9405-08

RR Swan Princess Funmeal Pack, 1994

❑ ❑	RR Sw9401	Puffin: walking figurine penguin	$2.00-4.00
❑ ❑	RR Sw9402	Jean-Bob: spinning top frog	$2.00-4.00
❑ ❑	RR Sw9403	Rothbart: w/ snap-on lion costume	$2.00-4.00
❑ ❑	RR Sw9404	Prince Derek	$2.00-4.00
❑ ❑	RR Sw9405	Princess Odette/Swan	$2.00-4.00

RR Sw9401-05

RR Nickelodeon School Tools Funmeal Pack, 1995

❑ ❑	RR Ni9501	Krumm Book Mark		$1.00-2.00
❑ ❑	RR Ni9502	Rocko Ruler		$1.00-2.00
❑ ❑	RR Ni9503	The Gromble Container		$1.00-2.00
❑ ❑	RR Ni9504	Spunky Container		$1.00-2.00
❑ ❑	RR Ni9505	Oblina Eraser		$1.00-2.00
❑ ❑	RR Ni9506	Ickis Pencil Holder		$1.00-2.00

RR Ni9501-06

Sbarro

Located within the malls of America, the Sbarro fast food restaurant chain serves up a menu of primarily pizza and salads. They started their kid's meal program in late 1998 and early 1999. Focusing their advertising on Garfield related merchandise, their kid's meal program involves a series of four toys and associated pizza box packaging.

SB Garfield Kid's Meal, 1999

❏ ❏	SB Ga9901	Pizza Puzzler: Garfield/gray	$3.00-4.00
❏ ❏	SB Ga9902	Pizza Puzzler: Garfield/pink	$3.00-4.00
❏ ❏	SB Ga9903	Pizza Puzzler: Garfield/yellow	$3.00-4.00
❏ ❏	SB Ga9904	Pizza Puzzler: Odie	$3.00-4.00

SB Ga9901-04

Sonic, America's Drive-In

Sonic's corporate headquarters in Oklahoma City, Oklahoma, maintain and franchise over 1,750 drive-in restaurants. Started in 1959, Sonic Drive-Ins offer an "old timey" approach to fast food service. Customers drive into one of twenty-four to thirty-six covered parking spaces and order made-to-order food through an intercom speaker system. The customer's order is delivered by a carhop, sometimes on roller blades. This approach is reminiscent of McDonald's 1950s approach to fast food delivery—only Sonic Drive-Ins offer made-to-order sandwiches and feature signature items such as Extra-Long Cheese Coneys, hand-battered onion rings, tater tots, Fountain Favorites, and the Sonic Wacky Pack for kids.

Delivering a specially designed premium or stock premiums from companies like Admark, Sonic Drive-Ins offered six to eight different Wacky Pack Kid's Meal programs a year in the early nineties. In the late nineties, when competition from other fast food restaurants became keener, the number of promotions doubled. In 1999, forty years after their beginnings, Sonic is still delivering a nostalgic "slice of American pie" with their highly differentiated quick-service delivery system. "Sonic, America's Drive-In" continues to promote family values and provide great kids' premiums throughout the 1990s.

1990s Sonic restaurant

SO Adventures of the Super Sonic Kids Wacky Pack Kid's Meal, 1990

❏ ❏	SO Ad9001	Corkey on Skateboard	$4.00-7.00
❏ ❏	SO Ad9002	Rick Holding Blue Skateboard	$4.00-7.00
❏ ❏	SO Ad9003	Brin in Pink Jogging Suit	$4.00-7.00
❏ ❏	SO Ad9004	Steve in Red Shirt/Blue Pants	$4.00-7.00

SO Ad9001-04

SO Jumpin' Jukebox Bank Wacky Pack Kid's Meal, 1990

❏ ❏	SO Ju9001	Jukebox Bank: yellow design	$7.00-10.00
❏ ❏	SO Ju9002	Jukebox Bank: red design	$7.00-10.00
❏ ❏	SO Ju9003	Jukebox Bank: green design	$7.00-10.00
❏ ❏	SO Ju9004	Jukebox Bank: blue design	$7.00-10.00

SO Ju9001-02

SO Bag-A-Wag Wacky Pack Kid's Meal, 1991

❏ ❏ SO Ba9101	Man on hamburger	$3.00-4.00
❏ ❏ SO Ba9102	Man w/ hamburger & bag of hamburgers	$3.00-4.00
❏ ❏ SO Ba9103	Man running/kneeling w/ bag of hamburgers	$3.00-4.00
❏ ❏ SO Ba9104	Man in hamburger vehicle	$3.00-4.00

SO Ba9101-04

SO Brown Bag Buddies Wacky Pack Kid's Meal, 1993

❏ ❏ SO Br9301	Brown Bag Man on skis	$3.00-4.00
❏ ❏ SO Br9302	Brown Bag Man on sled/brown	$3.00-4.00
❏ ❏ SO Br9303	Brown Bag Man on inner tube	$3.00-4.00
❏ ❏ SO Br9304	Brown Bag Man on snowboard/yellow	$3.00-4.00

SO Br9301-04

SO Holiday Express Wacky Pack Kid's Meal, 1993

☐ ☐ SO Ho9301   Engine $4.00-5.00
☐ ☐ SO Ho9302   Box Car $4.00-5.00
☐ ☐ SO Ho9303   Coal Car $4.00-5.00
☐ ☐ SO Ho9304   Caboose $4.00-5.00

SO Ho9301-04

SO Pull Back Flyers Wacky Pack Kid's Meal, 1994

☐ ☐ SO Pu9401   Two Engine Airliner $2.00-4.00
☐ ☐ SO Pu9402   Four Engine Airliner $2.00-4.00
☐ ☐ SO Pu9403   Blimp $2.00-4.00
☐ ☐ SO Pu9404   Shuttle $2.00-4.00
☐ ☐ SO Pu9405   Swept Wing Fighter $2.00-4.00
☐ ☐ SO Pu9406   Dual Tailed Bomber $2.00-4.00

SO Pu9401-06

SO Wacky Blasters Wacky Pack Kid's Meal, 1994

❏ ❏ SO Wa9401   Squirt Gun: yel w/ orange pump $2.00-3.00
❏ ❏ SO Wa9402   Squirt Gun: orange w/ yel pump $2.00-3.00
❏ ❏ SO Wa9403   Squirt Gun: pink w/ green trim $2.00-3.00
❏ ❏ SO Wa9404   Squirt Gun: green w/ pink trim $2.00-3.00

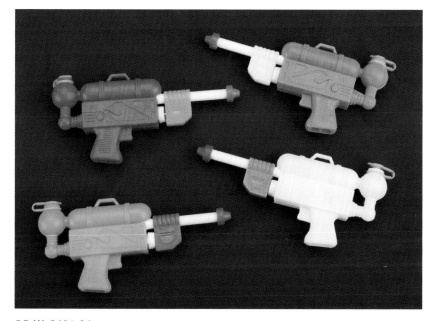

SO Wa9401-04

SO Airtoads Wacky Pack Kid's Meal, 1995

❏ ❏	SO Ai9501	Frog w/ Sunglasses	$2.00-4.00
❏ ❏	SO Ai9502	Frog w/ Purple Baseball Cap	$2.00-4.00
❏ ❏	SO Ai9503	Frog w/ Orange Polka-Dot Shorts	$2.00-4.00
❏ ❏	SO Ai9504	Yellow Spotted Frog	$2.00-4.00
❏ ❏	SO Ai9505	Frog w/ Powder Blue Shorts	$2.00-4.00
❏ ❏	SO Ai9506	Frog w/ Blue Shirt	$2.00-4.00

SO Ai9501-06

SO Wacky Robots Wacky Pack Kid's Meal, 1995

❏ ❏	SO Wa9501	Runaway Robot: purple	$2.00-3.00
❏ ❏	SO Wa9502	Runaway Robot: green	$2.00-3.00
❏ ❏	SO Wa9503	Runaway Robot: red	$2.00-3.00
❏ ❏	SO Wa9504	Runaway Robot: yellow	$2.00-3.00
❏ ❏	SO Wa9505	Runaway Robot: blue	$2.00-3.00
❏ ❏	SO Wa9506	Runaway Robot: black	$2.00-3.00

SO Wa9501-06

SO Back N Forth Racers Wacky Pack Kid's Meal, 1996

❑ ❑	SO Bf9601	Sports Car: yel chassis, blue frame	$2.00-3.00
❑ ❑	SO Bf9602	Sports Car: blue chassis, yel frame	$2.00-3.00
❑ ❑	SO Bf9603	Sports Car: pink chassis, grn frame	$2.00-3.00
❑ ❑	SO Bf9604	Sports Car: grn chassis, pink frame	$2.00-3.00
❑ ❑	SO Bf9605	VW: yel chassis, blue frame	$2.00-3.00
❑ ❑	SO Bf9606	VW: blue chassis, yel frame	$2.00-3.00
❑ ❑	SO Bf9607	VW: pink chassis, grn frame	$2.00-3.00
❑ ❑	SO Bf9608	VW: grn chassis, pink frame	$2.00-3.00

SO Bf9601-04

SO Spectrum Spirals Wacky Pack Kid's Meal, 1996

❑ ❑	SO Sp9601	Slinky: star shaped	$2.00-3.00
❑ ❑	SO Sp9602	Slinky: 6 sided	$2.00-3.00
❑ ❑	SO Sp9603	Slinky: heart shaped	$2.00-3.00
❑ ❑	SO Sp9604	Slinky: square shaped	$2.00-3.00
❑ ❑	SO Sp9605	Slinky: circle shaped	$2.00-3.00

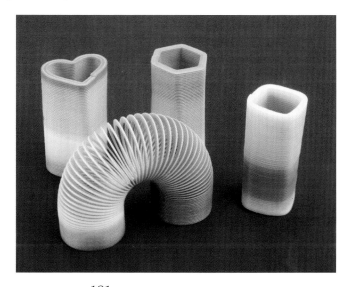

SO Sp9602-05

SO Hurl-A-Critter Wacky Pack Kid's Meal, 1997

❏ ❏	SO Hu9701	Stuffed Animal: Butterfly	$2.00-3.00
❏ ❏	SO Hu9702	Stuffed Animal: Lizard	$2.00-3.00
❏ ❏	SO Hu9703	Stuffed Animal: Lady Bug	$2.00-3.00
❏ ❏	SO Hu9704	Stuffed Animal: Frog	$2.00-3.00

SO Hu9701-04

SO Slush Squirters Wacky Pack Kid's Meal, 1997

❏ ❏ SO Sl9701 Squirter: Opal
    Orange $2.00-3.00
❏ ❏ SO Sl9702 Squirter: Betty
    Bubble Gum $2.00-3.00
❏ ❏ SO Sl9703 Squirter: Larry
    Lime $2.00-3.00
❏ ❏ SO Sl9704 Squirter: Cherry-O
    $2.00-3.00
❏ ❏ SO Sl9705 Squirter:
    Coconutty $2.00-3.00
❏ ❏ SO Sl9706 Squirter:
    Grapester $2.00-3.00

SO Sl9701-06

SO Wacky Chew-Chew Wacky Pack Kid's Meal, 1997

❑ ❑	SO Wc9701	Engine/Drink Car	$3.00-5.00
❑ ❑	SO Wc9702	Ketchup Car	$3.00-5.00
❑ ❑	SO Wc9703	Corn Dog Car	$3.00-5.00
❑ ❑	SO Wc9704	Hamburger Car	$3.00-5.00
❑ ❑	SO Wc9705	Hot Dog Car	$3.00-5.00
❑ ❑	SO Wc9706	Fries Car	$3.00-5.00
❑ ❑	SO Wc9707	Nuggets Car	$3.00-5.00
❑ ❑	SO Wc9708	Cheese Sandwich Car	$3.00-5.00

SO Wc9701-08

SO Zoops Wacky Pack Kid's Meal, 1997

❑ ❑ SO Zo9701 Animal Slinky: Hippo
$2.00-4.00

❑ ❑ SO Zo9702 Animal Slinky: Lion
$2.00-4.00

❑ ❑ SO Zo9703 Animal Slinky: Gator
$2.00-4.00

❑ ❑ SO Zo9704 Animal Slinky: Elephant $2.00-4.00

SO Zo9701-04

SO Chillin' Choo-Choo Wacky Pack Kid's Meal, 1998

☐ ☐	SO Ch9801	Engine: Banana split	$3.00-5.00
☐ ☐	SO Ch9802	Car: Sundae w/ choc. syrup/cherry	$3.00-5.00
☐ ☐	SO Ch9803	Car: Strawberry shake	$3.00-5.00
☐ ☐	SO Ch9804	Car: Ice cream cone	$3.00-5.00

SO Ch9801-04

SO Super Sonic Space Racers Wacky Pack Kid's Meal, 1998

☐ ☐	SO Su9801	Airplane: red	$2.00-3.00
☐ ☐	SO Su9802	Airplane: pink	$2.00-3.00
☐ ☐	SO Su9803	Airplane: blue	$2.00-3.00
☐ ☐	SO Su9804	Airplane: green	$2.00-3.00

SO Su9801-04

Subway

The rapid growth of Subway outlets in malls and strip mall centers has placed Subway in the forefront of fast food operations. Their kid's meal program, named Subway's Kids' Pak, began in earnest in 1993. However, the last five years of operation have not been smooth ones for Subway: many outlets are totally out of toys at times and several outlets within a specific geographical area could all be distributing different premiums. With the growth of diet conscience consumers, Subway's patrons appear to be young adults rather than children; consequently, the kid's meal program has gotten off to a rough start. Subway's Kids' Pak features Subway's five fresh vegetable characters, including Subway's Subman.

1990s Subway restaurant sign

SU Hackey Sacks Kids' Pak Meal, 1993

❏ ❏ SU Ha9301 Lenny Lettuce
$3.00-4.00
❏ ❏ SU Ha9302 Pappy Pepper
$3.00-4.00
❏ ❏ SU Ha9303 Pearl Onion
$3.00-4.00
❏ ❏ SU Ha9304 Petey Pickle
$3.00-4.00
❏ ❏ SU Ha9305 Tilly Tomato
$3.00-4.00

SU Ha9301-05

SU Doodletop Jr. Kids' Pak Meal, 1994

❏ ❏	SU Do9401	DoodleTop Jr. (blue)		$1.00-2.00
❏ ❏	SU Do9402	DoodleTop Jr. (blue)		$1.00-2.00
❏ ❏	SU Do9403	DoodleTop Jr. (purple)		$1.00-2.00
❏ ❏	SU Do9404	DoodleTop Jr. (red)		$1.00-2.00

SU Do9401-04

SU Explore Space Kids' Pak Meal, 1994

❏ ❏	SU Ex9401	Astronaut/2p		$2.00-4.00
❏ ❏	SU Ex9402	Space Shuttle		$2.00-4.00
❏ ❏	SU Ex9403	Lunar Lander/3p		$2.00-4.00
❏ ❏	SU Ex9404	Space Station/2p		$2.00-4.00

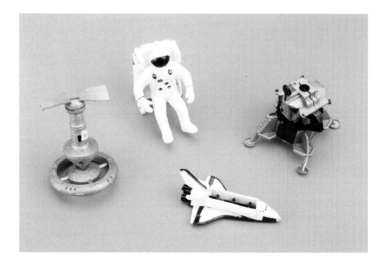

SU Ex9401-04

SU Inspector Gadget Kids' Pak Meal, 1994

❏ ❏	SU In9401	Stamp Pad	$3.00-4.00
❏ ❏	SU In9402	Surprise Squirter (purple)	$3.00-4.00
❏ ❏	SU In9403	Hidden Squirter (blue)	$3.00-4.00
❏ ❏	SU In9404	Magnifying Glass	$3.00-4.00

SU In9401-04

SU The Santa Claus Kids' Pak Meal, 1994

❏ ❏	SU Sa9401	Santa Cube Block Puzzle	$4.00-5.00
❏ ❏	SU Sa9402	Action Snow Globe	$4.00-5.00
❏ ❏	SU Sa9403	Elves Action Figure	$4.00-5.00
❏ ❏	SU Sa9404	Santa Claus Action Figure	$4.00-5.00
❏ ❏	SU Sa9405	U-3 Comet the Reindeer	$4.00-5.00

SU Sa9401-05

SU Bump In the Night Kids' Pak Meal, 1995

❏ ❏	SU Bu9501	Mr. Bumpy Figurine	$2.00-4.00
❏ ❏	SU Bu9502	Squishington (hollow)	$2.00-4.00
❏ ❏	SU Bu9503	Molly Figurine	$3.00-5.00
❏ ❏	SU Bu9504	Destructo Figurine	$2.00-4.00

SU Bu9501-04

SU All Dogs Go to Heaven 2 Kids' Pak Meal, 1996

❏ ❏	SU Al9601	Charlie: brown & tan, sitting	$2.00-4.00
❏ ❏	SU Al9602	Sasha: rust color, standing	$2.00-4.00
❏ ❏	SU Al9603	Itchy: brown w/ blue sweater	$2.00-4.00
❏ ❏	SU Al9604	Carface: gray, purple/black sweater	$2.00-4.00
❏ ❏	SU Al9605	U-3 David: boy standing	$2.00-4.00

SU Al9601-05

SU Dino Stompers Kids' Pak Meal, 1997

❏ ❏	SU Di9701	Triceratops		$2.00-3.00
❏ ❏	SU Di9702	Dimetrodon		$2.00-3.00
❏ ❏	SU Di9703	Parasaurosophus		$2.00-3.00
❏ ❏	SU Di9704	Tyrannosaurus Rex		$2.00-3.00
❏ ❏	SU Di9705	U-3 Dino (not a wind-up)		$3.00-4.00

SU Di9701-04

SU Blues Clues Kids' Pak Meal, 1998

❏ ❏	SU Bl9801	Birthday Blue		$4.00-5.00
❏ ❏	SU Bl9802	Mailbox		$4.00-5.00
❏ ❏	SU Bl9803	Tickety Tock		$4.00-5.00
❏ ❏	SU Bl9804	Handy Dandy Notebook		$4.00-5.00

SU Bl9801-04

Taco Bell

Taco Bell is owned by PepsiCo along with Kentucky Fried Chicken and Pizza Hut. This chain was founded in 1962 by Glenn Bell, whose early focus was geared toward the teenage market. The kid's meal program began in the eighties in conjunction with Hallmark collectibles. At that time, however, such collectibles were too far advanced for the consuming public. That is, kids were not primarily interested in Hallmark, because TV cartoon shows were more appealing.

In the nineties, Taco Bell introduced their own line of food characters: Taco Man, Cheddar Fred, Hedda Lettuce, and Tomato Red. These characters were intended to focus children's awareness on safety programs as well as on Taco Bell's food selections. When this advertising approach did not achieve success, Taco Bell shifted their kid's meal focus to more mature topics, leading to some very successful promotions. It wasn't until 1995 that Taco Bell selected the appropriate premiums for their consuming public; it was teenagers who were the consuming customers, not children, and teenagers were more interested in premiums like Mutant Jungle Mix-up, Star Wars, Tick, and/or Ace Ventura rather than stickers. By the late 1990s, Taco Bell was doing about six successful kid's promotions per year, the most popular of which was certainly the Star Wars promotion in 1999.

1990s Taco Bell restaurant

TB Desert Cruisers Kid's Meal, 1995

❑ ❑	TB De9501	Mo: pink car/green alligator/2p	$2.00-3.00
❑ ❑	TB De9502	El Sid: purple car/black bug/2p	$2.00-3.00
❑ ❑	TB De9503	Packrabbit: red car/yellow turtle/2p	$2.00-3.00
❑ ❑	TB De9504	Slob: blue jeep/orange fish/2p	$2.00-3.00

TB De9501-04

TB Flintstones Stone Age Stampers Kid's Meal, 1995

❑ ❑	TB Fl9501	Pebbles w/ regular stamp	$3.00-4.00
❑ ❑	TB Fl9502	Fred w/ rolling stamp	$3.00-4.00
❑ ❑	TB Fl9503	Barney w/ regular stamp	$3.00-4.00
❑ ❑	TB Fl9504	Dino w/ rolling stamp	$3.00-4.00
❑ ❑	TB Fl9505	U-3 Fred w/ no stamp	$3.00-4.00

TB Fl9501-04

TB Street Sharks Kid's Meal, 1995

❏ ❏	TB Sh9501	Fp: Big Slammu Jawsome Chopper/brn/wht	$2.00-3.00
❏ ❏	TB Sh9502	Ripster Gruesome Toothsome: blue/wht shark head	$2.00-3.00
❏ ❏	TB Sh9503	Squirter: Jab Street/4"/grayish	$2.00-3.00
❏ ❏	TB Sh9504	Streex Wrist Crunch'r: coin holder/wrist band	$2.00-3.00
❏ ❏	TB Sh9505	U-3 Fp: Gray Shark/rubber	$2.00-3.00
❏ ❏	TB Sh9506	U-3 Fp: Hammerhead Shark/rubber	$2.00-3.00

TB Sh9501-04

TB The Mask Kid's Meal, 1995

❏ ❏	TB Ma9501	Spin Top: Yellow "Somebody Sssss-top Me!"	$3.00-4.00
❏ ❏	TB Ma9502	Light Switch Cover: "It's Party Time"	$3.00-4.00
❏ ❏	TB Ma9503	Ooze 'N Foam Dough w/ grn wacky dough mold/2p	$3.00-4.00
❏ ❏	TB Ma9504	Pencil Toper: Milo (dog) w/ grn mask cover/2p	$3.00-4.00

TB Ma9501-04

TB The Tick Kid's Meal, 1996

❏ ❏ TB Ti9601 Arthur Gliding
Sidekick w/ wings
$3.00-4.00
❏ ❏ TB Ti9602 Charles The
Brain Child Toss 'N Catch
$3.00-4.00
❏ ❏ TB Ti9603 Sewer Urchin
Underwater Diver
$3.00-4.00
❏ ❏ TB Ti9604 The Tick
Balancing Superhero
$3.00-4.00

TB Ti9601-04

TB Ace Ventura Kid's Meal, 1997

❏ ❏	TB Ac9701	Nesting Pets: Penguin & Ace/2p	$2.00-3.00
❏ ❏	TB Ac9702	Unpredictable Ball: blue plastic ball/opens	$2.00-3.00
❏ ❏	TB Ac9703	Rainforest Runaway: Car Launcher/3p	$2.00-3.00
❏ ❏	TB Ac9704	For the Birds: Feeder w/ Ace/2p	$2.00-3.00

TB Ac9701-04

TB Batman & Robin Kid's Meal, 1997

❏ ❏ TB Ba9701 Crash Batmobile:
    car $2.00-3.00
❏ ❏ TB Ba9702 Botanical Trap:
    terrarium $2.00-3.00
❏ ❏ TB Ba9703 Batman on Ice:
    popsicle mold $2.00-3.00
❏ ❏ TB Ba9704 Portable Bat Signal:
    flashlight $2.00-3.00
❏ ❏ TB Ba9705 U-3 Mr. Freeze Sleet
    Shooter: squirter
        $2.00-3.00

TB Ba9701-05

TB Star Wars Trilogy Kid's Meal, 1997

❏ ❏	TB St9701	Millennium Falcon Gyro/3p		$3.00-5.00
❏ ❏	TB St9702	Magic Cube		$3.00-5.00
❏ ❏	TB St9703	Balancing Boba Fett/2p		$3.00-5.00
❏ ❏	TB St9704	Floating Cloud City/2p		$3.00-5.00
❏ ❏	TB St9705	Exploding Death Star Spinner		$3.00-5.00
❏ ❏	TB St9706	R2-D2 Playset: w/ Princess Leia/2p		$3.00-5.00
❏ ❏	TB St9707	Puzzle Cube		$3.00-5.00
❏ ❏	TB St9708	U-3 Yoda		$2.00-3.00

TB St9701-08

TB The Mask Kid's Meal, 1997

❏ ❏	TB Th9701	Putty Thing Fish Guy	$2.00-3.00
❏ ❏	TB Th9702	Pretorius Wind-up	$2.00-3.00
❏ ❏	TB Th9703	Whistling Spinning Top	$2.00-3.00
❏ ❏	TB Th9704	The Mask Flyer	$2.00-3.00

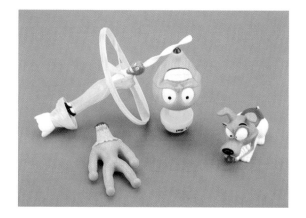

TB Th9701-04

TB Godzilla Kid's Meal, 1998

❏ ❏	TB Go9801	Tank	$2.00-4.00
❏ ❏	TB Go9802	Jet Fighter	$2.00-4.00
❏ ❏	TB Go9803	Godzilla	$3.00-5.00
❏ ❏	TB Go9804	Squishy Godzilla Egg: w/o Godzilla	$3.00-5.00
❏ ❏	TB Go9805	Squishy Godzilla Egg: w/ Godzilla	$3.00-5.00
❏ ❏	TB Go9806	Baby Godzilla	$3.00-5.00
❏ ❏	TB Go9807	Helicopter	$2.00-4.00

TB Go9801-07

Target

Food Avenues lead the way to Target's mini restaurants. Target discount stores are located in almost every state within the U.S., with the eastern United States lagging behind in retail outlets due to zoning regulations. In 1992, Target officially introduced their cast of characters called "The Targeteers." These characters, Ashley, Danielle, Buddy, and Ramon, consistently introduced Target's line of "Kids' Meal" promotions from 1992 through 1996.

From 1996 through 1998, the Target's Kids' Meal program ceased. Competition had taken its toll; discounters could no longer afford to compete with the national fast food chains. McDonald's began to move into discount stores like Wal-Mart, and even toward the end of 1998 this move forced the condensing of McDonald's operations from the non-profitable stores to the larger draw stores. Consumers were not coming to the discount stores for the kid's meal nor were they lingering at the discount stores long enough to shop and eat. Shopping was the main reason the store was utilized, and the "Target Food Avenue Kids' Meal" was out of step with nineties generation of shoppers. By 1998, Target had made attempts to revamp the kid's meal program, hoping to capitalize on leisure time shoppers.

1990s Target sign

TR Targeteers Kids' Meal, 1992

❑ ❑	TR Ta9201	Buddy w/ red car	$4.00-5.00
❑ ❑	TR Ta9202	Ashley w/ pink car	$4.00-5.00
❑ ❑	TR Ta9203	Danielle w/ blue car	$4.00-5.00
❑ ❑	TR Ta9204	Ramon w/ yellow skateboard	$4.00-5.00

TR Ta9201-04

TR Muppets Zing into Spring Kids' Meal, 1994

❑ ❑	TR Mu9401	Changeable Block: purple	$1.00-2.00
❑ ❑	TR Mu9402	Changeable Block: yellow	$1.00-2.00
❑ ❑	TR Mu9403	Changeable Block: green	$1.00-2.00

TR Mu9401-03

TR Targeteers Kids' Meal, 1994

❑ ❑	TR Ta9401	Ashley: blonde hair	$4.00-5.00
❑ ❑	TR Ta9402	Danielle: black hair w/ purple bow	$4.00-5.00
❑ ❑	TR Ta9403	Mei-Ling: black hair w/ red bow	$4.00-5.00
❑ ❑	TR Ta9404	Buddy: blue hat	$4.00-5.00
❑ ❑	TR Ta9405	Ramon: white hat	$4.00-5.00

TR Ta9401-05

TR Weiner Pack By Hillshire Farms Kids' Meal, 1994

❑ ❑	TR We9401	Weiner Man: blue hat/trunks w/ red shoes/3p	$4.00-5.00
❑ ❑	TR We9402	Weiner Man: yel hair/trunks w/ blk shoes/3p	$4.00-5.00
❑ ❑	TR We9403	Weiner Man: blk hair/red trunks w/ yel shoes/3p	$4.00-5.00
❑ ❑	TR We9404	Weiner Man: brn hair/blue trunks w/ wht shoes/3p	$4.00-5.00

TR We9401-04

TR Very Fast Food Kids' Meal, 1996

❏ ❏	TR Ve9601	Chessy: burger in red car	$3.00-4.00
❏ ❏	TR Ve9602	Fries: in green car	$3.00-4.00
❏ ❏	TR Ve9603	Drinkster: cup in yellow car	$3.00-4.00
❏ ❏	TR Ve9604	Hot Dogger: in blue car	$3.00-4.00

TR Ve9601-04

Wal-Mart

Wal-Mart is a discount chain led by Sam Wal-Mart. In the early nineties, the chain was just beginning to develop, so few kid's meal programs were offered. As the nineties grew, however, so did the number of Wal-Mart stores—soon McDonald's, the number one fast food chain in the industry, moved into prime Wal-Mart locations. This has lead to Exclusive McDonald's Wal-Mart Happy Meal Toys being given out only at Wal-Mart stores during 1997 and 1998.

1990s McDonald's Wal-mart sign

WM GI Joe/Potato Head Kid's Meal, 1993

❏ ❏	WM Gi9301	GI Joe: Bazooka	$3.00-4.00
❏ ❏	WM Gi9302	GI Joe: Grunt	$3.00-4.00
❏ ❏	WM Gi9303	GI Joe: Roadblock	$3.00-4.00
❏ ❏	WM Gi9304	GI Joe: Wet Suit	$3.00-4.00
❏ ❏	WM Gi9305	Potato Head Kid: Sabrina	$2.00-4.00
❏ ❏	WM Gi9306	Potato Head Kid: Slick	$2.00-4.00
❏ ❏	WM Gi9307	Potato Head Kid: Spike	$2.00-4.00
❏ ❏	WM Gi9308	Potato Head Kid: Tulip	$2.00-4.00

WM Gi9301-04

WM Gi9305-08

Wendy's

    Named after the founder's daughter "Wendy," these restaurants have flourished in the nineties. Started in 1969 by R. David Thomas as a single restaurant in Columbus, Ohio, Wendy's has grown to become the third largest hamburger chain in the United States, behind only McDonald's (#1) and Burger King (#2). Currently, however, Wendy's position is being challenged by Carl's Jr. through their acquisitions of Hardee's and Sandy's fast food restaurants. Wendy's provides an assortment of bags and boxes along with their premiums for the kid's market. Alf premiums led the early way for kid's marketing, with The Jetsons and sports meals right behind. Wendy's produces about six Kids' Meal programs a year.

1990s Wendy's restaurant sign

WE Alf Tales Kids' Meal, 1990

☐ ☐	WE Al9001	Alf as Aladdin on Magic Carpet	$2.00-3.00
☐ ☐	WE Al9002	Alf as Knight of the Round Table	$2.00-3.00
☐ ☐	WE Al9003	Alf as Little Red Riding Hood	$2.00-3.00
☐ ☐	WE Al9004	Alf as Romeo in Sleeping Beauty	$2.00-3.00
☐ ☐	WE Al9005	Alf as Third Pig of Three Little Pigs	$2.00-3.00
☐ ☐	WE Al9006	Alf as Robin Hood	$2.00-3.00

WE Al9001-05

WE Fast Food Racers Kids' Meal, 1990

☐ ☐	WE Ff9001	Salad Scrambler	$3.00-4.00
☐ ☐	WE Ff9002	French Fry Rider	$3.00-4.00
☐ ☐	WE Ff9003	Kids' Meal	$3.00-4.00
☐ ☐	WE Ff9004	Frosty Flyer	$3.00-4.00
☐ ☐	WE Ff9005	Single Sizzler Hamburger	$3.00-4.00
☐ ☐	WE Ff9006	Potato Peeler	$3.00-4.00

WE Ff9001-05

WE The Jetson's Space Gliders Kids' Meal, 1990

❏ ❏	WE Js9001	Fergie: on pink base	$2.00-4.00
❏ ❏	WE Js9002	Judy: on yellow base	$2.00-4.00
❏ ❏	WE Js9003	Elroy: on turquoise base	$2.00-4.00

WE Js9001-03

WE Yogi Bear & Friends Kids' Meal, 1990

❏ ❏	WE Yo9001	Yogi: on grn base w/ picnic basket	$2.00-4.00
❏ ❏	WE Yo9002	Snagglepuss: on blue base	$2.00-4.00
❏ ❏	WE Yo9003	Ranger Smith: in canoe on wht base	$2.00-4.00
❏ ❏	WE Yo9004	Boo-Boo: w/ pink shirt on gry base	$2.00-4.00

WE Yo9001-04

WE Wacky Wind-Ups Kids' Meal, 1991

❏ ❏	WE Wa9101	Burger		$2.00-4.00
❏ ❏	WE Wa9102	Frosty		$2.00-4.00
❏ ❏	WE Wa9103	Fries		$2.00-4.00
❏ ❏	WE Wa9104	Mealbox		$2.00-4.00
❏ ❏	WE Wa9105	Potatoes		$2.00-4.00
❏ ❏	WE Wa9106	U-3 Wacky Roller: purple cone		$2.00-4.00

WE Wa9101-05

WE Rocket Writers Kids' Meal, 1992

❏ ❏	WE Ro9201	Pen/Rocket: purple		$2.00-3.00
❏ ❏	WE Ro9202	Pen/Rocket: yellow		$2.00-3.00
❏ ❏	WE Ro9203	Pen/Rocket: pink		$2.00-3.00
❏ ❏	WE Ro9204	Pen/Rocket: green		$2.00-3.00
❏ ❏	WE Ro9205	Pen/Rocket: turquoise		$2.00-3.00
❏ ❏	WE Ro9206	U-3 Pen/Rocket: orange		$2.00-3.00

WE Ro9201-06

WE Cybercycles Kids' Meal, 1994

❏ ❏ WE Cy9401   Gryphon: gold $2.00-3.00
❏ ❏ WE Cy9402   Dragon: green $2.00-3.00
❏ ❏ WE Cy9403   Lightning: red $2.00-3.00
❏ ❏ WE Cy9404   Shark: blue $2.00-3.00
❏ ❏ WE Cy9405   Techno: purple $2.00-3.00
❏ ❏ WE Cy9406   U-3 Three Wheeler: blue/yellow $2.00-3.00

WE Cy9401-06

WE Cartoons Kids' Meal, 1996

❏ ❏ WE Ca9601   Split Apart Car: purple $2.00-3.00
❏ ❏ WE Ca9602   Convertible: green $2.00-3.00
❏ ❏ WE Ca9603   Hot Rod: red $2.00-3.00
❏ ❏ WE Ca9604   Police Car: blue $2.00-3.00
❏ ❏ WE Ca9605   U-3 Stretch Limo: yellow $2.00-3.00

WE Ca9601-05

WE Felix the Cat Kids' Meal, 1997

❏ ❏	WE Fe9701	Felix: plush/stuffed w/ yel jumpers/tongue showing	$3.00-4.00
❏ ❏	WE Fe9702	Shoe Laces: yellow w/ Felix name	$3.00-4.00
❏ ❏	WE Fe9703	3-D Mini Poster: paper	$3.00-4.00
❏ ❏	WE Fe9704	Catch Game: Felix w/ string/sphere w/ blue disc	$3.00-4.00
❏ ❏	WE Fe9705	Trophy: Felix on top of gold stand	$3.00-4.00
❏ ❏	WE Fe9706	U-3 Roller Fun Ball: sphere w/ Felix inside	$3.00-4.00

WE Fe9701-06

WE Sonic Cycles Kid's Meal, 1997

❏ ❏	WE So9701	Motorcycle: blue	$2.00-3.00
❏ ❏	WE So9702	Motorcycle: red	$2.00-3.00
❏ ❏	WE So9703	Motorcycle: silver	$2.00-3.00
❏ ❏	WE So9704	Motorcycle: copper	$2.00-3.00
❏ ❏	WE So9705	Motorcycle: green	$2.00-3.00
❏ ❏	WE So9706	U-3 Motorcycle: yel w/ blue rider	$2.00-3.00

WE So9701-06

WE On Wheels Kids' Meal, 1998

❏ ❏	WE On9801	Vehicle: Chicken Nuggets	$2.00-3.00
❏ ❏	WE On9802	Vehicle: French Fries	$2.00-3.00
❏ ❏	WE On9803	Vehicle: Drink	$2.00-3.00
❏ ❏	WE On9804	Vehicle: Hamburger	$2.00-3.00
❏ ❏	WE On9805	U-3 Frosty Truck: red w/ yel frosty	$2.00-4.00
❏ ❏	WE On9806	U-3 Circus Wagon: grn w/ a purple giraffe	$2.00-4.00

WE On9801-06

WE Snoopy & the Peanuts Gang Kids Kids' Meal, 1998

WE Sn9801-06

❏ ❏ WE Sn9801 Snoopy Etch-A-Sketch w/ blue pen/2p $3.00-4.00

❏ ❏ WE Sn9802 Snoopy Head: comic scenes $3.00-4.00

❏ ❏ WE Sn9803 Snoopy Doghouse: w/ scenes $3.00-4.00

❏ ❏ WE Sn9804 Snoopy on blue rolling wheel $3.00-4.00

❏ ❏ WE Sn9805 Snoopy w/ Woodstock light $3.00-4.00

❏ ❏ WE Sn9806 U-3 Snoopy in rolling yellow wheel $3.00-4.00

Whataburger

Whataburger is a privately owned chain of south and southwest Texas fast food restaurants that did not seriously enter the kid's meal premium market until the late 1980s and early 1990s. The chain of restaurants was started in 1956 in Corpus Christi, Texas, by Harmon A. Dobson and featured a unique A-frame roof designed to avoid hurricane damage in Texas communities.

Prior to 1990, most of Whataburger's premiums came from stock distributed by Admark and other standard premium vendors. In the 1990s, their focus changed and the number of kid's meals expanded. Their kid's meal is simply called a "Whataburger Kid's Meal" with a wavy "W" forming the company's logo and six characters representing the restaurant's appeal.

1990s Whataburger sign

WB Krazy Kritters Kid's Meal, 1996

❏ ❏	WB Cr9601	Stuffed Character: blu/yel elephant	$2.00-3.00
❏ ❏	WB Cr9602	Stuffed Character: yel duck	$2.00-3.00
❏ ❏	WB Cr9603	Stuffed Character: pink/yel pig	$2.00-3.00
❏ ❏	WB Cr9604	Stuffed Character: blk/wht panda	$2.00-3.00
❏ ❏	WB Cr9605	Stuffed Character: yel/grn mouse	$2.00-3.00
❏ ❏	WB Cr9606	Stuffed Character: grn/org dog	$2.00-3.00

WB Cr9601-06

WB Mini Speedsters Kid's Meal, 1996

❏ ❏	WB Mi9601	Car: silver	$2.00-3.00
❏ ❏	WB Mi9602	Car: metallic blue	$2.00-3.00
❏ ❏	WB Mi9603	Car: powder blue	$2.00-3.00
❏ ❏	WB Mi9604	Car: yellow	$2.00-3.00
❏ ❏	WB Mi9605	Car: black	$2.00-3.00
❏ ❏	WB Mi9606	Car: aqua	$2.00-3.00

WB Mi9601-06

WB Roarin' Racers Kid's Meal, 1996

❏ ❏	WB Ro9601	Yellow Whale	$1.00-2.00
❏ ❏	WB Ro9602	Green Whale	$1.00-2.00
❏ ❏	WB Ro9603	Orange Hippo	$1.00-2.00
❏ ❏	WB Ro9604	Blue Hippo	$1.00-2.00
❏ ❏	WB Ro9605	Aqua Gator	$1.00-2.00
❏ ❏	WB Ro9606	Purple Gator	$1.00-2.00

WB Ro9601-06

WB Watch Em Work Kid's Meal, 1996

❏ ❏	WB Wa9601	Pick up Truck: yellow wheels	$2.00-3.00
❏ ❏	WB Wa9602	Van: purple wheels	$2.00-3.00
❏ ❏	WB Wa9603	Volkswagon: green wheels	$2.00-3.00

WB Wa9601-03

WB Tiremaster Kid's Meal, 1997

❏ ❏	WB Ti9701	Green Tire		$2.00-3.00
❏ ❏	WB Ti9702	Yellow Tire		$2.00-3.00
❏ ❏	WB Ti9703	Red Tire		$2.00-3.00
❏ ❏	WB Ti9704	Blue Tire		$2.00-3.00

WB Ti9701-0

WB Winter Twisters Kid's Meal, 1997

❏ ❏	WB Wi9701	Slim (Santa Claus) Bendy		$2.00-4.00
❏ ❏	WB Wi9702	Sparky (Christmas Tree) Bendy		$2.00-4.00
❏ ❏	WB Wi9703	Chilly (Snowman) Bendy		$2.00-4.00
❏ ❏	WB Wi9704	Rudy (Reindeer) Bendy		$2.00-4.00

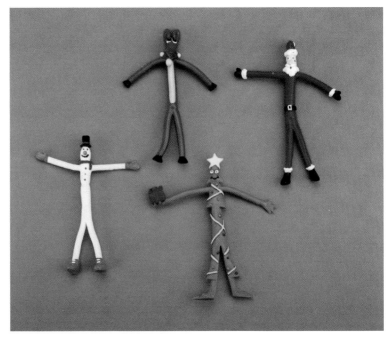

WB Wi9701-0

White Castle

White Castle is known as the world of Slyders! Established in 1921 in Wichita, Kansas, by E. W. Ingram and Walt Anderson, White Castle is recognized as the original fast food hamburger restaurant chain. It has remained true to its early advertising, using such slogans as "Buy 'Em By The Sack," "It's Like Nothin' Else, Nothing," "Slyders, The Taste Some People Won't Live Without," and "What You Crave."

Currently, White Castle has locations in Chicago, Cincinnati, Dayton, Columbus, Cleveland, Detroit, Indianapolis, Kansas City, Minneapolis, St. Paul, Louisville, Lexington, Nashville, New Jersey, New York City, St. Louis, and Philadelphia. Of the 297 total restaurants, however, only about 42 are distributing kid's meal toys. White Castle's cast of advertising characters, which originated in the eighties, includes Friar Wack, Princess Wilhelmina, King Woolly, Queen Winnevere, Sir Wincelot, Wendell, Wally, Willis the Dragon, Woofles, Woozy Wizard, Wobbles & Woody, and Wilfred. "The Castle Meal" is the name identifying a "Meal Fit for a Kid." The hamburgers are steamed on the bun with lots of onions added; in addition to being sold in the restaurants, they are frozen and shipped to local grocery stores along with the newly designed chicken sandwich and sold to "craving" customers in all fifty states. The kid's meal promotions were launched in 1986 with a special Indian hat that read: "ME BIG CHIEF!—BUY ONLY WHITE CASTLE ALL-BEEF HAMBURGERS."

In the early nineties, White Castle's cast of advertising characters changed to four Castle Dudes, characters based on food products. This restaurant chain typically features six "Castle Meal" promotions for kids per year, marking most of the premiums with their "White Castle" logo. By 1998, White Castle was only distributing kid's meal toys in two major markets, the Chicago and Indianapolis regions.

1990s White Castle restaurant

WC Castle Meal Friends Castle Meal, 1990

❏ ❏	WC Ca9001	Wendell	$4.00-5.00
❏ ❏	WC Ca9002	Sir Wincelot	$4.00-5.00
❏ ❏	WC Ca9003	Woofles	$4.00-5.00
❏ ❏	WC Ca9004	Princess Wilhelmina	$4.00-5.00
❏ ❏	WC Ca9005	Willis	$4.00-5.00
❏ ❏	WC Ca9006	Woozy Wizard	$4.00-5.00
❏ ❏	WC Ca9007	Game: Feast—Secret Room	$4.00-5.00

WC Ca9001-07

WC Fat Albert & The Cosby Kids Castle Meal, 1990

❏ ❏	WC Fa9001	Fat Albert	$15.00-20.00
❏ ❏	WC Fa9002	Russell w/ yel scarf on flat sled	$15.00-20.00
❏ ❏	WC Fa9003	Donald w/ grn sweater on traditional sled	$15.00-20.00
❏ ❏	WC Fa9004	Harold standing on snowboard	$15.00-20.00

WC Fa9001-04

WC Castle Friend Bubble Makers Castle Meal, 1991

❏ ❏ WC Bu9101   Bubble Blower: Sir Wincelot $4.00-5.00
❏ ❏ WC Bu9102   Bubble Blower: Woozy Wizard $4.00-5.00
❏ ❏ WC Bu9103   Bubble Blower: Princess Wilhelmina $4.00-5.00
❏ ❏ WC Bu9104   Bubble Blower: Wendell $4.00-5.00

WC Bu9101-04

WC Tootsie Roll Express Castle Meal, 1992

❏ ❏ WC To9201   Train Car: Engine in red $5.00-7.00
❏ ❏ WC To9202   Train Car: Coal Car in turquoise $5.00-7.00
❏ ❏ WC To9203   Train Car: Box Car in purple $5.00-7.00
❏ ❏ WC To9204   Train Car: Caboose in red/green $5.00-7.00

WC To9201-04

WC Wind-Up Castleburger Dudes Castle Meal, 1992

❏ ❏	WC Wi9201	Castleburger Dude	$4.00-5.00
❏ ❏	WC Wi9202	Castle Drink Dude	$4.00-5.00
❏ ❏	WC Wi9203	Castle Fry Dudette	$4.00-5.00
❏ ❏	WC Wi9204	Castle Cheeseburger Dude	$4.00-5.00

WC Wi9201-04

WC Castle Meal Friends, 1993

❏ ❏	WC Me9301	Friar Wack	$4.00-5.00
❏ ❏	WC Me9302	King Wooly & Queen Winnevere	$4.00-5.00
❏ ❏	WC Me9303	Wally	$4.00-5.00
❏ ❏	WC Me9304	Wilfred	$4.00-5.00
❏ ❏	WC Me9305	Wobbles & Woody	$4.00-5.00

WC Me9301-05

WC Castle Meal Express Castle Meal, 1994

❑ ❑	WC Ex9401	Train Car: Engine in blue	$5.00-7.00
❑ ❑	WC Ex9402	Train Car: Box Car in green	$5.00-7.00
❑ ❑	WC Ex9403	Train Car: Coal Car in red	$5.00-7.00
❑ ❑	WC Ex9404	Train Car: Caboose in green/blue	$5.00-7.00

WC Ex9401-04

WC Hammerman Castle Meal, 1994

❑ ❑	WC Ha9401	Bath Sponge	$4.00-5.00
❑ ❑	WC Ha9402	Soap	$4.00-5.00
❑ ❑	WC Ha9403	Toothpaste: pink bubblegum w/ pink brush	$5.00-8.00
❑ ❑	WC Ha9404	Tooth Paste: blue grape w/ blue brush	$5.00-8.00

WC Ha9401-04

WC Oreo Bendable Castle Meal, 1994

❏ ❏ WC Or9401   Oreo
Bendy w/ cookies
$3.00-5.00

WC Or9401

WC Key Racers Castle Meal, 1995

❏ ❏ WC Ke9501	Car: orange van	$2.00-4.00
❏ ❏ WC Ke9502	Truck: turquoise pickup truck	$2.00-4.00
❏ ❏ WC Ke9503	Car: purple car	$2.00-4.00
❏ ❏ WC Ke9504	Car: yellow VW	$2.00-4.00

WC Ke9501-04

WC Puppy in My Pocket Castle Meal, 1995

❑ ❑	WC Pu9501	St. Bernard & Gray/White Shaggy Dog	$2.00-4.00
❑ ❑	WC Pu9502	Collie & Black/Tan Dog, sitting	$2.00-4.00
❑ ❑	WC Pu9503	Cocker Spaniel & Black/Tan Terrier	$2.00-4.00
❑ ❑	WC Pu9504	Blue Poodle & Tan Bulldog	$2.00-4.00
❑ ❑	WC Pu9505	White, Black Face & Tan/White Dog, sitting	$2.00-4.00
❑ ❑	WC Pu9506	Fox Terrier, laying & Tan Dog w/ raccoon eyes	$2.00-4.00

WC Pu9501-
06

WC Silly Squeeze Squirters Castle Meal, 1995

❑ ❑	WC Si9501	Squirter: Woofles (purple)	$3.00-5.00
❑ ❑	WC Si9502	Squirter: Woozy Wizard (blue)	$3.00-5.00
❑ ❑	WC Si9503	Squirter: Willis (orange)	$3.00-5.00
❑ ❑	WC Si9504	Squirter: Wilfred (green)	$3.00-5.00

WC Si9501-04

WC Mini-Plush Castleburger Dudes Castle Meal, 1998

❏ ❏	WC Mi9801	Castle Fry Dudette	$4.00-5.00
❏ ❏	WC Mi9802	Castle Drink Dude	$4.00-5.00
❏ ❏	WC Mi9803	Castleburger Dude	$4.00-5.00
❏ ❏	WC Mi9804	Castle Cheeseburger Dude	$4.00-5.00

WC Mi9801-04

Index